Acorns

Stories and Poems from

The Joined-up Writers Group

Valley Publishing

First published by Valley Publishing in 2006

꙳

ISBN 0-9554572-0-3

ISBN 978-0-9554572-0-3

Cover photograph by Maureen Nicholls
Printed in Great Britain by Sebright Printers, Bristol

Contents

Title	Author	Page

New Beginnings

Ann Merrin

New beginning? It wasn't something she'd ever thought about. She'd had lots of new beginnings in her youth, but for the last fifty years life had trundled along the tracks laid down by previous generations. And it hadn't been at all bad.

Jane was seventy-two last birthday. They'd had a bit of a 'do'. The kids had hired St. John's church hall and had laid on a lovely spread. About eighty people turned up – mostly family. The music was a bit loud at times but Jane had enjoyed the dancing.

That was in January. Who would have thought such a short time would bring so many changes?

The week after the party had been bitterly cold and by the weekend snow had disrupted everyone's life. Jane had managed to get to the Post Office on Monday and was feeling quite pleased with herself as she carefully picked her way back along the salted pavement.

The sky was leaden and the road looked wet where the gritter had spread its load. But the road wasn't wet, it was icy and as the blue car came round the corner it slid gracefully toward where Jane had stopped – transfixed. She couldn't hurry away on the treacherous pavement, and she *shouldn't* stay and wait for the car that was heading towards her. A blind panic took over and she lunged into the snow-clad hedge behind her. Her wide eyes met those of the driver as his car glided into the hedge. It pinned her legs to the spiky bush and a searing pain shot up her right leg into her hip.

Everything stopped. Jane couldn't move. The car engine was switched off. There was an overwhelming silence. A stillness. And then, all at once: noise, people, shouting, animated faces. She sank to the ground.

Some hours later Jane awoke. She recognised the feel of those smooth sheets and the distinctive smell you only find in hospitals. She moved her head slowly and was pleased to see Sheila and her husband, John, sitting beside the bed.

"Wh-what…," her voice trailed away.

"It's alright Mum. You've had a lucky escape. Just one leg fractured. They've set it and checked you all over while you've been out of it!"

"What time is it?"

"Half past two. Neil and Janice are on their way over. Are you hungry?"

"No, no. I feel a bit sick. I think I could manage a cup of tea though."

Jane turned her head away from her daughter and came face to face with a stranger. There was something familiar though. Those eyes.

"I'm Bill – the car driver. Just wanted to make sure you were ok."

"Bill came in with you. He's been here since eleven. Would you like some tea too Bill?"

"Well, no. I'd better be going. Now that I know you're ok."

"Oh, do stay for a cuppa. I'd really like to know what happened. I seem to have a series of still photographs parading slowly through my head."

So Bill stayed and explained how the car took to the ice and left his control.

He visited her daily and when she left hospital, he was the one to drive her home. Sheila and Neil thought it very amusing that their mother should have a 'man friend'. Though, on a more serious note, they liked Bill and had noticed a bloom in Jane's cheeks that they hadn't seen for many years.

So in a way the accident had been a new beginning. Jane had found a new friend. Bill became a regular visitor. Not only was he helpful when she wasn't so mobile, but he was a good listener and understood her insecurities when she wondered if she would ever walk out of her own front door again. He made her laugh too – how long it had been since she'd shared some fun.

But she **had** gone out of her front door again. The summer had found them taking regular day trips. They enjoyed visiting garden centres and stately homes. They'd joined a dance class too, so there were several trips to weekend dance venues.

Now here she was, the day before her wedding. She had been speechless when Bill proposed. Who would have thought anyone would contemplate such a major 'new beginning' at the age of seventy-two? Yet Jane felt sure that she was heading into the best time of her life.

Mayday Proposal

Patricia Welford

May I walk you to the Green?
May I watch you in the dance?
Maypole ribbon; hand clasped around.

May I walk you home again?
May I kiss your rose blessed lips?
Beloved you, my May Queen crowned.

May I ask you, be my Bride?
May I plead you don't say 'no'?
Come lie with me upon the ground

May I love you all day long?
May I share with you our child?
My love it swells for you profound.

May I love you when we're old?
May I love you 'til I die?
May I?

Ruby's Legacy

Patricia Lloyd

Fairworth Hall
Larksby
County Durham

10 November 1889

Dear Daisy

It is with great sadness that I have to tell you that Ruby has died. She gave birth to a little boy on Friday at 7.p.m. and died shortly afterwards.

The child was delivered safely, but it was a problem detaching the placenta that caused complications.

I know it will also be a shock to you that Ruby has had a child. She did not tell me until it became obvious. The mistress was very kind and allowed her to work right up to when her pains started. The local birthing nurse was called and the baby was born in Ruby's attic room in the master's house.

I have no idea who the father of her child is. Ruby did not venture far, having just one day off a month. The only place she visited was your home and that, not often, because of the long walk over the mountain.

I would much rather have come to give you this terrible news in person, but arthritis in my knees means that I cannot walk far nowadays.

Could you let me know the arrangements you will make with regard to the funeral of your daughter and also the future care of your grandson. Be assured I will do all I can to help, but as you know it is difficult for me (as companion to Lady Fairworth) to take too much responsibility.

Her Ladyship has allowed me to send a footman with this message. He will be able to wait for your reply.

With sincere condolences

Patience.

Brickwork Cottages
Dukestown
County Durham.   11 November 1889

Dear Patience

Thanks for letting me know about our Ruby and I am truly sorry. However, I am not taking responsibility for Ruby or her child. Why should I? You must know that Ruby is not my child. I can't believe that mother kept this from you all these years.

Ruby is the offspring of a dalliance between our father and another woman. Ruby was left with Father shortly after she was born. Her mother left to catch a boat to America with a fellow who had an interest in the gold rush. As far as I know, neither has been heard of since. Ruby was not your niece, she was your half-sister. Father paid Charlie and I to take her on. We had been married about a year and because we were living in Dukestown, Father thought it would be easy for us to pass her off as ours.

The money was useful and helped us put a home together. After a while, when our own kiddies were born, she became just like one of our own.

The day I took in Ruby was the last day I saw our mother. She has never forgiven me for helping Father. What was I to do? I was 19 years old, newly married and more or less told to take the child by Father.

Did you not ask yourself why I was not at his funeral? Mother did not let me know. I got the news from the local traveller when he called with our winter supply of wood.

Just who the father of the baby is, I do not have to work hard to guess. When Ruby came home to visit she talked all the time about Albert her "cousin". Perhaps you should have a long talk with that boy of yours. It seems to me that the child could be your grandson as well as your half-nephew.

Well now, you and mother can take some responsibility for our half-sister and her son. I loved Ruby but because I am in such financial straits what with Charlie being out of work and only one of our lot working, I cannot fund any funeral or wet nurse for the baby.

You go and see Mother, and perhaps between you, you will be able to give to Ruby just as I did for 14 years before she went into service. It's your turn now – yours and Mother's.

Your sister

Daisy

Fairworth Hall   12 November 1889
Larksby
County Durham

Dear Daisy

I was shocked and saddened by your letter. I really had no idea of Ruby's parentage. I truly always thought she was your's and Charlie's daughter. She was a good girl; kind and thoughtful and talented in the ways of keeping house. I thought she took after you.

Lord Fairworth called me into his study this morning and told me that he and Lady Fairworth had had a long discussion with Ruby when she first told them of her condition. Did you know that Ruby knew who her real parents were?

Well apparently she informed Lord and Lady Fairworth. It now transpires that since then, Lord Fairworth has been tracing Ruby's mother.

Incredibly, Mary Jenner is now living in Blackwellgate, Darlington. She is known as Lady Mary Forsyth-James. She returned from America with a large fortune. She made the fortune herself apparently, (by dubious means), about which Lord Fairworth did not expand. She has also acquired a poor but titled husband and incredibly, the marriage appears to be a happy one.

The offshoot of all this is that Mary Jenner (as she will always be known to me) is to collect the child and rear him as her own. Which, of course, he is, being her grandson.

In the meantime I have financed the provision of a wet-nurse and am glad to say that the baby is healthy and happy.

With regard to the baby's father you were right, it is Albert. I spoke to him immediately I read your letter. In fact I showed it to him. He said that he and Ruby enjoyed their time together, but so far as he was concerned he did not think the relationship had a future. Albert has now disappeared. I don't know whether to be pleased or sad. I am still angry and disappointed at the way he has behaved and feel glad to be rid of him. On the other hand, as his mother, I miss him and am concerned for him. No doubt he will turn up. Bad pennies usually do don't they?

Now to discuss Ruby's funeral. I have contacted all concerned (including our mother) and have arranged for Ruby to be buried here in Larksby. She was happy here and had many friends within the estate. The funeral is on Friday at 11.a.m. Lord and Lady Fairworth are to provide a luncheon in the church hall following the funeral.

Daisy, please come – you and Charlie. You were everything to her and she loved you. Our mother will also be here and she so much wants to see you again. It was Ruby's birth that caused the estrangement. Can some good come from her death – can it lead to reconciliation? I truly hope so.

With love

Patience

Behind the Beaded Curtain

Barbara Calvert

I never visited Madam Maria;
never passed through her beaded curtain;
never crossed her palm with silver,
or let her gaze on mine.
Those were my lines,
and I would find my way.
I could plot my own trail;
follow my own path.
The choices would be mine.

No map can show the way
to an unknown destination.
Here are your many options.
How will you proceed?
Flip a coin for fame and fortune;
self or selfless, love or lust.
How many times we think,
'Suppose it had gone the other way'.
But there is no way to unpick life's thread;
to begin again on a new design.

Now, if it were possible
I would enter her mystical cavern
and ask if her crystal ball
could look into the past.
I would study the paths I took,
and those I left behind.
Could she resist a knowing smile?
'I might have helped you
find your way.'

Secret Mission

Jane Mason

The full moon lit the landscape, allowing the group to see as if it was day. The leader quickly ushered the others towards the clearing in the woods. Finally they were able to rest, away from the fierce fighting continuing about a mile behind them. The muffled sound of gunfire sharpened their wits to remind them of the tasks that lay ahead.

All were new to this and had not been in France since before the beginning of the war. Even the trees were alien, menacing, as if whispering to them to go home, saying, "it's dangerous here".

Jeanne checked her shoes. The heels were intact, concealing her package. As a secret operative, of French parentage and with dark brooding looks, she would blend easily into this besieged land to do her bit for the war effort.

Emerging from the woods, the leader furnished them with up-to-date local intelligence and wished them all good luck as they disappeared to various prearranged destinations. Jeanne's heart beat a swift rhythm in her breast as she fervently prayed to meet no Germans this fine evening. She shivered with apprehension and perhaps a little fear.

Arriving in the small village, Jeanne knocked three times on the weathered brown door. A grey-haired woman, who said, "Good evening, the moon is bright tonight," slowly opened the resistance safe-house door.

Jeanne replied: "Safe and high in the sky."

Entering the candle-lit room Jeanne saw two men seated at the farmhouse table. They offered her a glass of wine, which she gratefully accepted, and welcomed her. She finally felt free from harm.

Jeanne's remit was to stay at the house until daylight and then move to a more remote location in the nearby countryside. She was to travel by horse and cart with a local Farmer who would collect her from the end of the road. For now Jeanne relaxed with these comrades, who were pleased to see her assisting them with their efforts against an unwanted occupier. They lifted their glasses to freedom and drank deeply of the homemade wine.

Seated at the front of the old cart in the morning Jeanne thought the road the roughest she had ever travelled and full of potholes. She was sure her backside would be covered in bruises by the time she reached her final destination. The Farmer didn't smell too pleasant either, a mixture of stale Gauloise cigarettes and cow muck.

Arriving at the farm, Jeanne was struck by its French rustic charm, being long and low-lying. This was going to be home for several weeks until her mission was completed. The farmer's wife showed Jeanne to her room above the barn, where a radio already resided, carefully hidden in an old wardrobe.

At nightfall Jeanne tapped a coded message into the radio, to alert England that she had arrived safely. She had learnt Morse code in training, whilst hidden away in Scotland. The quick response showed they had received it.

Jeanne settled into her idyllic country life very well and enjoyed waking up to the sound of the feisty cockerel announcing that morning had arrived, whilst protecting his girls in the hen house.

Several nights later a man, unknown to Jeanne, visited the farm asking to see her. "You have something I want," he said.

" What might that be?" she questioned.

"It's better you don't know," responded the unshaven man, "Just hand over the film."

"How do I know I can trust you?" she replied, instinctively knowing she could. Without further ceremony the man tipped Jeanne into the hay and removed both of her brown, lace-up brogue shoes. Using a penknife, he carefully slit open both heels of the shoes and removed his prize. "What a gentleman you are," said Jeanne.

"That I'm not," he answered, placing a full kiss on her upturned lips, before taking off into the black moonless night.

Jeanne was bewildered by the ruffian's approach but also fascinated, after all she was English and men didn't normally behave like that towards her. English manners didn't allow for it. Still, there was a war on and French men probably took their pleasure where they could get it.

A fortnight later, Jeanne was able to radio England to advise them that the rail link carrying German soldiers between two towns had been disabled. She prayed the man who had removed her shoes was safe.

Jeanne need not have worried - Pierre was hiding out in the local Champagne caves, carved into the hillside many years ago, together with his resistance comrades. He remembered the brave, stoic English woman and was intrigued by her courage in coming to France. Once things had died down a bit, after the direct hit at German operations, Pierre was planning an impromptu visit to the farm.

However, before he could visit her again, Jeanne was arrested by the Gestapo and sentenced to death. The resistance members couldn't let her die - this was not her country, she knew nothing and had refused to confess any involvement in the recent explosion. Brute force had been used but she had betrayed no one. Unfortunately the special pill she had hidden on her body had been found when they searched her and so suicide had not been an option.

As the firing squad lined up, Pierre hid amongst the crowd gathered to watch the morbid spectacle. These prisoners were giving their lives for France and he could only look on as Jeanne's body convulsed and died swiftly. Two tears slid silently down Pierre's saddened face as he crossed himself.

Blooming Marvellous

Naomi Stride

If a scientist claimed that they had invented a pill that helped combat obesity and osteoporosis, could guard against depression and at the same time unite communities and help combat global warming, people would be clambering over each other to be first to try such a miracle product. No such product has yet been invented, but there is a pastime that can make all these claims.

I grew up with a gardener. I remember watching my Dad bent double planting out rows of seedlings, nurturing them, feeding them, watering them, talking to them and gently blowing away bugs with smoke from the pipe that was always clenched between his teeth. It didn't matter what the weather did (which is probably just as well in England) if it was the right time of year to plant out, prune, cultivate or harvest, then that was what he would be doing.

He still does it now, at 73, and must be one of the fittest O.A.P's that I know. He has two allotments as well as tending the gardens for "the old folk" in his village. I used to admonish him for not "exercising" in the conventional sense, until I realised that with his daily timetable of mowing lawns, digging and planting he was burning off in excess of 1500 calories a day—equating to three hours in a gym—and he was out of doors taking advantage of the fresh air and sunlight.

As a boy growing up during the Second World War, Dad's family was encouraged to Dig for Victory. The Germans had disrupted trade into Britain and consequently food rationing was introduced. If, however, families and communities could grow as much of their own food as possible, it would ensure adequate nutrition. People were united in their fight against the Germans and if they could not be on the front line, they would show their support by digging their gardens.   It is possible that my Dad's love of gardening was instilled through "Digging for Victory" during childhood. Indeed he still does "Dig for Victory" but now the victory he craves is a little more peaceful.

Each year his local village hosts a Flower Show, which he looks forward to with relish. For the past five years Dad has reigned supreme, winning most of the flower trophies with his Sweet Peas (his favourite plant) and several other prizes for his vegetables.   The competition, although fierce, is usually friendly with most of the exhibitors gladly sharing their tips for producing the best possible specimens of plants or vegetables.   Dad, for instance, swears his success is down to the dead sheep buried beneath his allotment!

But however friendly the competition, there is an eagerness to win. People will tweak and polish their produce until they look perfect. Chrysanthemums are groomed with cotton buds to ensure all the petals are facing the same way, onions are woven together into elaborate plaits, yellow buckets filled with water are hidden beneath tables to lure the dreaded pollen beetle away from prized blooms.

There have been stories of rivals interfering with prize leeks before competitions, deflowering blossoms and stealing marrows. Competitors have been known to jump on each other's exhibits in a disgraceful show of un-sportsman-like behaviour, whilst others have been disqualified after it was discovered that they had bought the blooms that won them the coveted cup.   However this behaviour is rare, and generally horticultural shows are a festival of bonhomie, uniting gardeners and promoting a wonderful sense of satisfaction and well-being for the exhibitors.

Showing is an added bonus for the seasoned gardener. The real benefit has to be the satisfaction of growing and ultimately harvesting your own produce. Last year from May to December, Dad lived off his allotment, hardly needing to purchase any more fruit or vegetables. He grew 50 lb of gooseberries, 35 lb of raspberries, 80 lb of tomatoes, 25 lb of potatoes and countless (but not weightless) other vegetables. Anything he cannot use is either given away to grateful family members, or swapped with neighbours on the allotment promoting a sense of camaraderie between gardeners.

He can also bathe in the knowledge that he is doing his bit to help save the planet. His produce has not travelled miles to end up on his plate and his plants absorb carbon dioxide, replacing it with much needed oxygen, helping to balance out the greenhouse effect.

There is no doubt that gardening is good for you. It can burn off as many calories per hour as swimming or jogging. It can help guard against osteoporosis by exposing the skin to vital Vitamin D provided by the sun (make sure you use adequate sun screen and pop on a hat). It can boost your self-esteem and help promote a wonderful sense of satisfaction. It can also bring people together and it may help to save the planet.

However, with people living ever-busier lives few people spend much time in their gardens, let alone grow their own vegetables. Garden space is given up to conservatories, decking and patios with a token pot or two overflowing with bedding plants. The pressure being put on Local Governments to produce new housing could also be a reason why the number of allotments has fallen from 1,400,000 at its peak during the War to a mere 250,000.

With the news being inundated with stories of obesity, the escalating costs of depression and the horrendous effects of global warming, the Government needs to introduce new strategies to help combat these problems, or perhaps they could reuse old ones. Promoting gardening could provide a much needed solution. If the Government reintroduced its "Dig for Victory" campaign and promoted horticulture, whether in your own back yard or allotments, it could be the answer to a better and longer life.

Snake Oil Can Kill

Phil Whitehead

Uncle Harry should not have died, or so most people thought. "He would be alive now if he hadn't gone into hospital," said sister-in-law Brenda, and Jimmy thought there was some truth in that. At eighty years of age, Harry had still been a prolific walker, not your marathon man in joggers and iPod on the hip, just a simple, walk-the-dog walker every day, rain or shine, for three hours at least, on the mountainside nearby. It wasn't his dog; he wasn't allowed one in his small flat in the sheltered accommodation where he lived. It was his friend John's dog, which was good in a way; at least the dog still had a home.

Then, on a cold, bleak, February day, Harry had got out of bed and his legs had collapsed under him. He had crawled to the phone and called John to say he might be late. John called the warden and they both entered the flat. Harry's body was twisted on the floor and he was trying to rub some sort of oil in the base of his spine. "Rub it in there," he had said to John, "That usually works." But it didn't. The ambulance was called. Harry went to hospital, or more precisely hospitals; you could have had a T-shirt engraved with "Harry's 2005 Hospital Tour" on it. Not one Consultant could diagnose the cause of his collapse and Harry ended up in that hilltop cottage hospital for the elderly, which smelled of urine and decay, where the only route out was in a box. Three months later, shrunken in size and the will to live, Harry died of a heart attack trying, for one last time, to get back on his legs again. At least that was the diagnosis, but the autopsy had shown up a small indent in the base of Harry's spine. It

21

was not considered the cause of his death; could it have stopped him walking? No one was sure, but John recalled Harry rubbing oil there several times in recent years, it had clearly given him pain.

There was a rush to clear Harry's flat; there were plenty of oldies waiting to occupy it as the flats were well heated. There was little of value in it and most things went to charity. For old time's sake, Jimmy was given a small, well-travelled brown case with a box of personal items, some clothing and newspapers in it. Sarah, Jimmy's wife, wondered why he had bothered; they just ended up in the attic with the relics from other dead relatives' houses. And there they would have remained, if it wasn't for Harry's will. Although his chattels were almost worthless, he was a canny saver, but his will, written many years before, left half his money to a woman in Alabama, USA. There was uproar. After all, hadn't his own family cared for him all those years? But the will held and the family of a Precious Williams, deceased, gratefully accepted eight thousand pounds having no idea why a "honky" in England should care to leave money to a poverty-stricken, black Alabama family.

Nor did Jimmy, but was there a clue to this mystery in the stuff he had? He was determined to investigate. One Saturday afternoon, when Sarah and his daughters had gone to town shopping, he retrieved the suitcase from the attic. Opening the box inside it, he found a small, cylindrical, cream pomander with a painting of a camellia on the lid. He opened it and sniffed the interior. He recoiled; it was not the pot-pourri he had expected, rather the fading smell of camphor oil. The only other item in the box was an old, white china bottle. On the side it said in faded black letters: "Clark Stanley's Snake-Oil Liniment, Selma AL. Accept no substitutes." He pulled out the china stopper and breathed in the fumes. His reaction was violent. This really was camphor oil or mostly so. The bottle was about one quarter full. Was this the oil Harry had relied on so much, using the pomander? He shook his head and looked at its base. There, visible under strong light, was scratched the name *Williams*. Wasn't this the surname of the woman from Alabama in the will? And come to think of it, he recalled from his frequent business trips to the USA that all States had a state flower, and the camellia was the State Flower of Alabama. The findings disturbed him. He remembered that many years ago Harry had emigrated to America, and that he had intimated at tough times out there, but when questioned he literally clammed up and changed the subject.

Then, from the suitcase Jimmy removed what turned out to be the inner pages of some Alabama newspapers; the Selma Times, the Montgomery Courier and the Birmingham Gazette. All were dated early August 1954. They were clearly kept for a purpose, and one which became horrifyingly clear as he read them. Each one had a picture and graphic description of the lynching by "persons unknown", but having all the hallmarks of the Ku Klux Klan, of a thirty five year old Negro, Elmore Williams, of Selma, the previous Saturday night. Apart from stringing him up from a tree at his home, the murderers had robbed and burned down his home. His wife, Precious, and their five children had fled to relatives. It appeared that his crime had been to exercise his democratic right and register to vote at an up-coming State election. The papers all expressed the view that the perpetrators were unlikely to be caught. Was Harry involved? Jimmy daren't believe it, but then, Harry did return home late in 1954! Maybe Harry's will was an act of contrition, if it was, would it be enough?

Gingerly, Jimmy looked in the case again. The clothing inside was white and felt like it was made of fine cotton. He had not seen anything like the first item he withdrew; It was a robe with wide, short sleeves. He held it to him. It came just to his knees. He put it on the bed then withdrew the next item.

The hairs on his head stood high. It was the pointed hood of a Klan member, with those sinister triangular eye- holes and a red cross on the front. He didn't know what to do. It was getting dark outside. Sarah would be home in about half an hour. Should he tell her? And then, something drew him inexorably to the idea that he should try it all on. He slipped on the robe and the hood and stood before the full-length bedroom mirror.

What happened next is only Jimmy's version; no one else can confirm it. *"I stood in front of the mirror and stared through those evil eye-holes. Suddenly a vision appeared before me, a group of men in white robes and hoods - the Klan. A tall, burning cross lit up the night and they were all chanting. I seemed to have a rope in my hands and I was reaching out and hauling a tall Negro, his hands tied behind him, over the branch of a tree. He was screaming for mercy; I could see the whites of his eyes, they were almost popping out. Then, he was swinging free of the ground. I tied the rope to the tree. He was spinning, lurching and kicking out in frantic death-throes. As I turned away from the horror of it all, I felt a sharp pain in my lower back, as if I had been kicked hard. I collapsed on the floor, I couldn't get up, my legs were useless."* When Sarah and his daughters returned home about a half hour later, they found Jimmy on the bedroom floor with the robe still on him, his torso twisted as he tried desperately to rub some foul smelling oil from a pomander into the base of his back. The hood lay discarded at his side.

An ambulance was called and Jimmy was rushed to hospital, or more precisely hospitals, you could have had a T - shirt engraved with "Jimmy's 2006 Hospital Tour" on it. Not one Consultant could diagnose the cause of his collapse. Eventually, Jimmy ended up the youngest patient ever in that hilltop cottage hospital for the elderly, which smelled of urine and decay, where the only route out was in a box. Three months later, shrunken in size and the will to live, Jimmy died of a heart attack trying, for one last time, to get back on his legs again. The autopsy showed nothing unusual, although there was an indentation at the base of his spine which Sarah said she had not noticed before.

Search the internet and it will tell you that snake oil can sometimes kill, or was it Precious exacting a fitting revenge? The truth will never be known.

Spring

Ann Merrin

MARCH

Cold winds, bare branch trees

Look closely at the small buds

Turning gently green

APRIL

Bulbous flowers bloom

Full of enthusiasm

Attacked by harsh winds

MAY

Spring is here at last

Joyous month when warmth returns

To the soil and soul

smaller members of my audience. Lily, although sleepy, was still awake and listening.

"Come on Gramps, enough of the history, it's time to get to the interesting bit."

"The interesting bit, hmm." I looked out across the moonlit fields and remembered how, as a young man in my twenties, the history I was relating was still being lived, in spades. Here in the south, racism was rife and the Klu Klux Klan was not a figment of anyone's imagination, least of all for my family. But we survived and so did the plantation until 1915 when the dreaded boll weevil arrived. Crops across the state were halved, workers migrated and few survived the depression which followed.

I took up the story for Lily in the year 1925. I'd lost both parents, most of the field hands had left to try for work in the city and I was struggling to make the best of Pa's last big decision before his death; the planting of Sea Island cotton; it gave the best possible grade yarn and fetched double the price if you could get it right but was much harder to harvest.

"It was on a night just like tonight," I continued to Lily. "I was swinging through the fields, knowing we must escape weevils and hurricanes if we were to keep going and wondering all the time how in hell I was going to get help with the harvest. Since Ma and Pa died, I'd had no chance to go socialising and couldn't invite anyone home with the place in the state it was with no servants in the house.

I was tired and so lonely that as I walked the fields to inspect the cotton, I wept like a baby. Turning the corner of the bottom field I came face to face with a vision. Hell, I thought I was dreaming, or hallucinating. There, in between the rows was the most beautiful girl I've ever seen. The moonlight shining on her face, gave it a pearly sheen, I couldn't tell if she was white or black. Her hair was loose, hanging to her waist and she wore a long white shift thing with, well…I swear she had nothing underneath except her birthday suit, even her feet were bare. "

"Oh my, what did you do Gramps?" Lily was looking up at me, eager to know the truth, but there was no way on God's earth I could relate the full story to this young innocent. And If I did, I'm not sure she would believe me; truth is, I'm not sure I believe it myself, even now.

My mind went back to that night when, without a word she had come towards me, her arms open wide. She took my face in her hands pulling it down until her soft lips touched mine. I felt her mouth open as she pressed against me, her hands moving like the wings of a moth, fluttering up and down my body until I stood before her, naked as the day I was born and so hot with lust I could hardly breathe. I reached for her and she came, as ready and willing as I was. The white shift falling from her shoulders caught like a snowflake on her breasts and, just like a snowflake, melted at my touch. I watched in wonder as it fell to the floor, revealing beauty such as I had never seen. I kissed the soft underside of her arm resting around my neck, her skin was like silk and I was afraid to touch her with my big callused hands so using my lips instead, I caressed and explored the secret places; she responded with soft moans and we sank to the floor on a bed made from our discarded clothing, utterly lost to the world, consumed by the slow, heated passion of our lovemaking and the utter joy of dual release.

I looked down at Lily, still waiting expectantly for the dénouement of my story. "Well, I kissed her," I said hurriedly, "and then she disappeared. Next day was Sunday and I thought I'd better go to church and pray to be a better person. On the way out, the Pastor shook my hand and introduced me to his niece who was visiting from out of state. It was my Cotton Angel but she pretended we had never met. She shook my hand and looked up into my face, as innocent as you please."

"I believe we've already met," I mumbled. I had real trouble keeping my voice steady and my face was on fire.

Cool as a cucumber she shook her head. "Oh no, I'm sure I would remember. My Uncle tells me you are looking for help with the harvest. I've travelled down with six brothers all looking for work and all big and strong. Would you have anything to offer them?"

"I tell you Lily, if I hadn't already kissed her the night before, I reckon I would have done so right there and then in front of the Pastor. She sure as hell was turning out to be a real Cotton Angel."

"But you married her Gramps, didn't you ever talk about it afterwards?"

"No never! It was like I'd imagined the whole thing." I still puzzled about that.

"I don't remember Granny, was she really so beautiful?" Lily's voice was wistful.

I looked out over the cotton fields, still glowing in the dark. "Oh yes." I replied softly. "The most beautiful woman I ever saw." I smiled down at Lily. "And you are just like her. Now, go to bed and take these two sleeping little bodies with you. I'm going to sit a while and maybe…dream a dream."

Wedding Report, from "Witch" Magazine.

Philip Whitehead

The bride and the groom had been soul mates,
Who met at a ghost writing school.
He was a spook who was writing a book,
And she was a wicked young ghoul.

Transylvania was the only location,
That suited their devilish need.
And Halloween night was diabolically right,
To consummate their evil deed.

And so, on the stroke of midnight,
In a crypt by a tomb with a view,
In Dracula's lair, he married the pair,
And mingled the blood that he drew.

The bride wore a sheath of black velvet,
From the nape of her neck to her toe.
The bridegroom, in red, had two horns on his head,
The whole scene had a satanic glow.

The bridesmaids were all so bewitching,
A coven of friends of the bride.
But beware of these ladies, their heredity's Hades,
They would give you a hell of a ride!

And that best man so seemingly sanguine,
With the cute little curl on his forelock.
Watch out for his hoodoo, the guy's into voodoo,
I was told that he's really a warlock.

So I dined with the heinous couple,
Devilled kidneys were served *a la grecque,*
The *entre* was belated whilst the steaks were cremated,
But magic mushrooms encouraged the *craic.*

Bloody Mary's were served as the cocktail,
Though the coffee I fancied the most.
In a hint to the tragic, it was laced with black magic,
And evil spirits were served for the toast.

So if you're well into the occult,
And this wedding just gets you excited,
Find those of your set, out there on the net,
At *www.fiendsreunited.*

PF

Alan Beckett

Blue birds in childish dreams enshrined,
In an arboreal circle, deep among the roots of the mind.

Trees sigh and breathe in a far brooding forest,
Seeking the astral child, inner hearts open to caress.

The three legged eye sees all, never a lie,
When on the peripheral, brownies may fly.

No matter your faith in Heaven or in Hell,
No matter your fear, be where the tiny spirits dwell.

In the flicker of an eyelid and the darting of a bee,
With trust and belief the portal shall open for thee.

Summer Swell

Alan Beckett

Number fifty-one Crowndale Crescent lay at the bottom of a small valley in a quiet, middleclass suburban neighbourhood. Conservatively painted and pointed, the property was resplendent with a large lawn, an ornamental pond and an exemplary rose garden. It was a hot summer afternoon in July, after many such days during a long dry spell. Nothing much moved inside the house and all was quiet. Too quiet.

The only residents at home were Sodface, the Jack Russell, Bakebean, the ginger tomette, the gerbil twins, Pinky and Perky and Ying and Yang, the goldfish. Cosmic the parrot, who preferred to be alone, was in the lounge counting his feathers. The owners, Mr and Mrs McCavity were away for the day visiting their outlaws.

The lounge clock had just chimed two o'clock when there was a muffled thump somewhere below ground followed by a deep, long vibration. In the kitchen, Sodface instantly picked up this seismic event. His back leg twitched, his left ear shot up and a half hearted huff emanated from his throat.

Across the kitchen Bakebean opened one eye, yawned and went back to sleep. Pinky and Perky continued to scratch furiously at the plastic walls of their tank when they suddenly noticed Bakebean. She had now opened both eyes, had sat up and was staring directly at them whilst running her tongue seductively over her teeth.

Ying and Yang registered the subterranean event by swimming around their fish tank much faster and in the opposite direction, and finally, Cosmic the parrot responded by saying "What do you call that?" mimicking Mrs McCavity's voice. Imitating Mr McCavity's voice he quickly followed this with, "Pretty boy".

Meanwhile, just below Mrs McCavity's award winning rose beds something dark and ancient was on the move. It stirred, it grew and swelled, displacing earth, stones and slithering creatures as it forced its way upward. An amorphous life form from the depths was transcending its subterranean lair and seeking domination of the surface.

Inside it was siesta time. Not much moved in the house. The still warm air had lulled all the furry and feathery residents of the house back to nap central. Finding it hard to ignore the strange vibrations, Ying and yang had adopted a different strategy and had decided to swim back the other way but this time a bit slower thus taking in the asymmetrical ambience of the kitchen and to consider its unperturbed occupants. They were particularly interested in Bakebean and her singular fascination with the two furry fish in the tank on the dresser.

Outside the kraken whooshed and heaved. Flowerbeds became swirling dervishes of disturbing colour as its fiendish energy cast aside in just mere seconds, what had taken weeks of painstaking effort by Mrs McCavity to keep the borders and lawns immaculately trimmed and manicured. Every blade of grass in its place and every square foot of soil sanitised of weeds and all ghastly crawling things that had got on her plants as well as on her nerves.

This destroyer of worlds, this dweller of the deep had no respect for keeping up appearances and could not give a monkeys about any floral aspirations Mrs McCavity may have had. Winning the WI flower show with her prize roses meant as much to this cleaving behemoth as a bull might consider the Ming dynasty when trashing a china shop.

The roses were the next to hit the air as it surged relentlessly on towards the house. But when throwing its gyrating body up against the structure of the building it suddenly encountered resistance. No weak, crumbling soil or superior multi-purpose compost with added nutrients and trace elements to push aside, but the brick and mortar construction of a 1950's detached des-res with large twin bay windows and a double garage.

It hesitated, backed off, swirled around in frustration seeking the smallest crack to gain entry. It ran back over the garden as surges of power piled up on itself, its rage increasing by the second. Confined by the elevated sides of the garden it gathered strength to break the solid walls standing in its way.

As it rose in anger, it was steadily compromising the houses defences and gaining entry wherever it could.
The airbricks and cracks in the wall, the extractor fan and every bit of plumbing going through to the kitchen. It had consolidated its body so massively that its sheer size had now completely engulfed the garden.

Inside the house, Sodface, with his superior hearing and sniffing facilities had sensed that something big was going down, and being forever the vigilant and stout-hearted protector of Fifty One Crowndale Crescent, he had legged it upstairs.

However, Bakebean, had taken the view that if Sodface had lost his bottle and had retreated to the wardrobe then, always the opportunist, this was the ideal time to move in on Pinky and Perky. She jumped onto the dresser and went into stalk mode just as the first snaking tendrils of the Kraken slithered silently across the new floor tiles, recently imported from Mexico, costing Mr McCavity £15 a tile.

From their vantage point in the corner of the kitchen, Ying and Yang observed that too many bizarre happenings were taking place at once. So they decided to change their direction again but this time swim backwards so that they could review and carry out a more in-depth analysis of the strange occurrences before they got screwed by them.

Pinky and Perky were still oblivious to the swirling monstrosity slithering past below them. Instead the gerbil twins were looking straight up into the grinning, lip licking face of Bakebean as she dithered on a somewhat moot point as to which furry morsel was the first one to join her organisation.

The gerbils just sat there, entranced, paws hanging down like a couple of limp-wristed fashion executives. They were also insensible to the ruin and destruction of Mrs McCavity's eighteenth century crockery as it leapt off the lower shelves in a beautifully executed choreography of antique spinning plates and dishes. Each one succumbing to the rippling musculature of the force sweeping them aside.

Eventually Pinky, being the slightly more intellectual of the two, twittered to Perky along the lines. "Just keep smiling mush, it might confuse her."

But at that instant Bakebean was swept away and was too busy trying to deal with the smothering embrace of the Beast, than to indulge in any pre-apocalyptic snacks.

Punching their fists into the air in triumphant relief, Pinky and Perky were ecstatic until suddenly their tank swung round knocking them both to the ground. They too were on the move as the monster lifted their home off the dresser, heaving its way through the house, trampling everything in its path.

Next was the fish tank. As it toppled over pouring out its contents, a curious thing occurred to Ying and Yang. Having had years growing up in their tank and discovering and mapping their moderate but bijou universe, postulating hypothetical models and formulating equations as to how it got there, who put it there and above all was there really a unified theory of tanks giving; they were both suddenly teleported into a place that no longer had the confines of their neat and well understood universe.

Instead as the great Beast carried them and the others to oblivion, Yang reflected on how was it that suddenly the universe had expanded and was moving in just one direction. Could this be the fabled new age of aquarium and would they both have to return to the drawing board to recalculate their equations again. A very dark matter indeed.

Cosmic the parrot, who was looking straight ahead at the in-pouring of the monsters body through the broken lounge windows, observed its slimy tentacles snapping below his high perch. But Cosmic was not that bothered. He had seen this sort of thing before on the 'box' and the victims always got airlifted and rescued in the end. He would wait.

"Pretty boy," he squawked nonchalantly, but this profound utterance was drowned out by the rising cacophony below him. "Where's that bloody Sodface?" he added, as his stand was mercilessly swept from under him forcing him to make like a common budgie.

In the meantime, Sodface had ventured from the wardrobe and had tiptoed to the top of the stairs. He stood there trembling, just in time to see his fellow residents shoot past on the back of the beast. He mustered his deepest, fiercest bark and let it have it between the eyes; except it didn't have any. But this did not deter Sodface one iota. He went down a few steps nearer to the monster preparing to give it his loudest, most bloodcurdling howl. Unfortunately it just came out as a choked squeak instead.

Cosmic heard the squeak. There were no helicopters in sight yet so he decided he would have to use his wing-things again and fly up-stairs to speak to the dog about his appalling street cred. "What a drag," he squawked.

With the front door ripped off its hinges, much of Mr and Mrs McCavitys intimate belongings were now on public display as they moved slowly up either side of Crowndale Crescent. Most were tumbling around under the swirling body

41

of the monster, but lighter things like clothing, a lucky tank of gerbils and pieces of paper moved at a more leisurely pace.

As Pinky and Perky floated by, a water board engineer bent down to pick them up. He placed the tank in the back of his van along with a wet and miserable Bakebean curled up in the corner. She was really glad to see her little friends again. It perked her up no end as she licked her lips and smiled broadly at them.

As the fire brigade and more water company vehicles arrived to tackle the worst mains burst in the area for a century, one piece of paper, recently thrust through Mr and Mrs McCavity's letterbox, warned of imminent hose pipe bans, standpipes and a danger of severe drought, it being their duty to conserve water etc. But no one saw it, not even Ying and Yang. They were too busy exploring their expanded universe and trying to decide which way to swim round fifty-one Crowndale Crescent.

Look To The Future

Ann Merrin

Clarice looked at the future
Not in a ball or a magic lake
She saw it in her living room
And in her HEAD for pity's sake!

People would come to her back door
To ask for a reading or a sign
She'd sit them down and hold their hands
And tell them that things would be fine.

She had these guides who helped her out.
They talked to her, she said.
Told her things she couldn't know
And it was all inside her head.

A man turned up one evening
Said he'd come about his wife.
Clarice had him sitting down,
Told him things about his life.

She had a message from his wife.
The guides had passed it on.
But Clarice didn't say a word.
She'd be glad when he was gone.

She told him that his wife was fine
And happy where she was.
He smirked a bit, got up to go,
Said he had to catch his bus.

Clarice couldn't sleep that night.
She'd heard from his wife alright.
Heard how he'd bashed her head in
And stowed her body out of sight.

She needed help from her guides now.
She felt threatened by that man.
They told her where the wife was,
And that she should make a plan.

There was only one solution.
The police must be involved.
She phoned them in the morning.
Here was a murder to be solved.

She arranged where she would meet them:
A wood, quite close to her own home.
The police arrived at half past ten
But Clarice was dead and gone.

That man had lain in wait for her
And bashed her head in – what a cur!

SHE HADN'T SEEN <u>THAT</u> COMING!

The Music Room

Alan Beckett

A small room as silent as a country afternoon suddenly deserted of musician and tune. Carpets chequer its polished wooden boards, strewn around in a testimony of panic. Ancient opulence from the brass handled door to the flower tiled bricks.

A small fire licked and spat in its grate. An old French clock ticked on the mantle piece, heavy and ornate. A double bass stood proud and wooden. The music in its strings waiting to be bidden.

A mahogany dining table half draped in fine lace. Wineglasses balanced on its scarred face. Lipstick and blood smudging their organic stalks. A small caged bird makes a muffled squawk, too eager to talk.

Dreamy steam oozed from a silver samovar, still warm just like workers surround the queen of the swarm. Bone china cups and saucers attend its gargantuan base, with little plates of cakes, half eaten, littering the place.

A fly settles on a chocolate éclair. No one there. No one left to care. A music stand has fallen, collapsed across the floor. Sheets of music flap by the open veranda door.

Two flutes and a violin thrown together on the chaise-longue, mourning the passion of their lost players song, tapping the genius of the master folk. Bach, Chopin, Dvorak, each wedded to music and hope.

All are conspirators, code makers and code breakers. The music serves the people. The people serve the takers. The Parisian skyline is bled by the Sun. Blood red shadows flood askew, creeping down the scrolled balcony darkening the verandas view.

As the cold-hearted night descends, jackboots click in the cobbled streets below. A chilling wind blows. The fire in the grate flares, then dies back to a dull glow. The instruments of reason melt together, indistinguishable in the gathering gloom. The beast has entered the music room.

Lifefile I went to him and gave him a long kiss. We stood for a while just holding each other. Then I took Charles into the hall where it was quiet and where Janey and Roddy could meet their father. Charles died in an accident when Janey was six months old and Roddy two years.

Our children could not have had any idea that they would meet him when they arranged our return to the party. I could not explain to Charles why I wanted to be alone with him and I could not talk to the children in front of their father. I could however, ensure they had some time with us both.

Charles and I sat on the stairs (our favourite place in my crowded home) and talked. We talked about our forthcoming marriage, the tiny ancient house we had bought and our future together. Lifefile, Charles looked at me and said,

"In a few years we will have children. A boy first of course, followed by a girl."

I laughed and said, "You can't plan these things you know."

He then gave me a present. In silk-lined individual boxes I found two long-stemmed deep red roses made of porcelain. Charles told me that I was to keep them always as a sign of his eternal love.

We were not allowed too much time in the hall – we were dragged back into the crowded noisy rooms full of family warmth.

Towards the end of the evening, as usual, we gathered around the piano and sang together while Mum played. We sang nursery rhymes for the kids, folk songs and Charles Wesley hymns for the rest of us.

After a while, Roddy and Janey came to me and told me we had to leave as our time was nearly up. I kept it casual Lifefile – the parting. I gathered the children to me and walked quietly out of the back door while the rest of the family were singing. My heart was breaking but I could not make a thing of kissing them all goodbye (especially Charles) because they would not understand.

As the time machine took off I was comforted knowing that I was leaving them all at a happy time in their lives. As we travelled back I pulled my children into my arms and thanked them for a truly miraculous and wonderful day.

Lifefile there was just one more thing I needed to do tonight before the children went to sleep. I called them into my bedroom, opened two long narrow boxes and gave Roddy and Janey a beautiful long-stemmed red rose with love from their father.

Lifefile I have to turn you off now. I need to lie down and re-live this very special day. Perhaps quiet will help me to come to terms with letting go of the past. Perhaps my children's greatest present to me is the realisation that my past has been a strong foundation from which I can move forward confidently into the future no matter what it might bring.

Roots

Phil Whitehead

Gethin pulled in at the roadside and got out of the car. Below him the river Taff twisted and curled its way through the base of the valley, the hazy afternoon sun tingeing it a silver-grey. It was so much cleaner than when, in his youth, twenty or so coalmines had all emptied their foul detritus into it, so blackening and polluting the water that no fish could survive in it. On the steep slopes opposite, rows of terraced houses sat firmly on ledges hacked out of the rock a century before. Most had been extended to encroach on their long, steep, narrow gardens to provide all modern facilities, paid for by wages earned prising coal out of the reluctant, unforgiving coal seams of the Rhondda. There was no smoke billowing out from shared chimney stacks as there used to be, but with no fires to light from the free coal that was a miners' right why should there be? The coalmines had long gone, even the tall, sinister black headstocks with their rapidly spinning wheels had been dismantled. In singer Max Boyce's apt words, "The pithead baths is a supermarket now."

Scanning the crests of the mountains Gethin noted the coarse grass covering the old, obscene waste tips, and hardy fir trees spreading out in all directions, imparting a distinctly Nordic feel to the hilltops. Lower down, the deciduous woodlands he so remembered as his childhood venture playground had thrived and spread out. Now, in late October, the trees were shutting down for winter, the foliage reddening and the leaves being let go until spring. There were a lot fewer pigeon lofts too; just the occasional brightly coloured shelters standing out from the landscape, and from only one had a flock of birds been released to fly joyously in ever-faster circles in the unbounded exercise yard of the sky.

He was here for the funeral of his cousin Jack, a top-flight economist in Welsh government, struck down by a heart attack at the age of fifty-five whilst on E.U. business in Brussels. The service was to be held in Jack's small terraced house, his wife refused to move from the Rhondda, and then at the cemetery on the hillside opposite. That had certainly grown in size, but then, as his favourite cousin Sissy had wryly remarked, "There's a lot of people around here dying to get in there." Gethin drove down to the narrow street alongside the river where Jack had lived. He parked some distance away and walked to the house. The front door was open. Inside was a sea of mourners in black, mostly middle aged and elderly women. Jack's coffin lay on a wheeled bier in the small front parlour. He studiously avoided it, preferring instead to remember him as he had last seen him in his posh Cardiff office, shown in by Jack's charming Personal Assistant.

He briefly embraced Jack's widow, Margaret and the two children. They had rarely met; Gethin, an inveterate drinker, was definitely not on her approved list. She was teetotal and a cold fish, much taken with the restrictive religion of a small Welsh nonconformist church. When he had once told her that he was an agnostic, she had said, somewhat disingenuously; "Well, I've not heard of that one, but I suppose we all worship the same God." Then, luckily, short, plump Sissy took his hand, led him to a corner of the living room and proffered a cup of tea which he gratefully accepted. "You're lucky you didn't have a wasted journey," she said laconically. "We nearly postponed the funeral. No ham in the Co-op for the sandwiches afterwards. You can't have a funeral without ham can you? I had to send our Bill all the way down to the new Tesco's in Porth." She looked up for a reaction. He grinned involuntarily, as he always did when Sissy spoke.

With five minutes to go to "Kick-off" as Sissy put it, a large contingent of men arrived, many of them Jack's workmates. Enviously he smelled the beer on their breath; they obviously knew Margaret's house rules. Shortly, the preacher, a tall, thin, unhappy, sixtyish man in a black suit and tie appeared, clutching a Welsh Service book. Briefly offering condolences, he led the way into the parlour for the service. Gethin stayed in the lounge, but the high voice, dramatically emphasized by the musicality of the Welsh language, carried to all. Jack got a brief mention at the beginning and then at the end of the service, but it was mostly a eulogy to Jesus and God, punctuated by many "Amen's". Together they sang the hymn "Calfaria", harmonizing gloriously; then, to the words of "The Lord's Prayer" in Welsh, the preacher preceded the coffin, with one simple wreath on top, to the hearse. With the precision honed on much practice, the coffin passed through the front door on the final "Amen." The men, quietly contemplative, filed out behind, this church did not allow women at the graveside.

At the steeply-inclined, wind-blown cemetery, the coffin was lowered into the ground. Jack's assistant Neville stood next to Gethin. As they filed past the open grave they noticed a woman, mid forties, slim, attractive high cheek bones and short, highlighted hair, wearing a long, elegant, fur-collared black coat, standing discretely by. She held a spray of flowers before her and she seemed familiar. Neville inclined his head towards her and she, noticing, dipped hers. "That's Megan, Jack's P.A." he whispered, "They've been lovers for years. She was with him in his room in Brussels when he died – smiling, I heard! Still, when you think of that old sourpuss down there, can't blame him can you?" Gethin shook his head ruefully. It would have been easy to say; "That's Jack, forever Jack the lad!" but he held fire. He just thought of the hurt his own infidelity had caused.

Then, all the mourners returned to Jack's house for a respectable interval, and to eat the ham sandwiches so diligently prepared. Shortly, the men took their leave. The name of the pub they were leaving for was dropped to Gethin. He was tempted, but returning home to his new partner suddenly seemed more important. He sought out Margaret to say goodbye. Sissy was also leaving; she held Margaret's hands in hers and was saying: "Well, Margaret, did you enjoy the day?" Out on the street, Gethin looked at the house opposite, which was where he had been born and had grown up. His roots were undoubtedly here, but today he knew a branch of his family tree had been severed.

His Blue Striped Boxer Shorts

Jane Mason

Maggots crawled over and around an inert body, secretly hidden away among sand dunes at the back of the deserted beach. Seagulls wheeled curiously overhead checking out a large mammal lying dead amongst the soft blonde grains. Rigor mortis had set in and thanks to recent humid weather the ample white marble skin was deteriorating fast.

How much longer before someone found this disgusting example of death? Would the body have putrefied, prior to some kind soul reporting its appearance to the Police? Thick grasses grew amongst the dunes helping to disguise Bob's last resting place. He was finally tranquil. The tide restfully ebbed and flowed, displaying plenty of ocean treasure at a tide line further down the beach.

Several months previously Bob and Sandra had retired from their city life and relocated to the seaside, to live out their final years quietly together. As house prices were exorbitant on the coast, they had downsized to a two bedroomed bungalow from their five bedroomed house in Gloucestershire. Selling their well-loved artifacts had been a chore, but necessary to begin their new life in Somerset.

There were no roses round the doorway or cottage garden, but a lovely seaside panorama could be surveyed from every window at the front of their new home. Sandra busied herself joining the local WI and helping out at a nearby playgroup, leaving Bob to potter happily around their new home and garden. It was tedious though compared to his old life. He'd left his lifelong mates behind and felt unable to saunter down to the local, for a pint of beer and a chat, as he didn't know anyone. He felt like a branch chopped from an old apple tree in flower. He then discovered the Internet.

Whilst planning their move away, friends had insisted they obtain an e-mail address to keep in touch. Bob had attended a free computer course for beginners at the college and purchased a computer to contact his many friends. Of course over time he'd begun surfing the World Wide Web and being of an inquisitive nature had discovered the seedier material lurking to be explored. Whilst Sandra was busy making jam, Bob was amusing himself watching Lusty Laura slither up and down her pole enticingly to an erotic dance tune.

Sandra casually mentioned one day, "You're spending an awful lot of time on that computer of yours. Anything interesting I should know about?"

"I shouldn't think so," replied Bob, "I'm just doing some research on historical web sites, to learn more about the neighbourhood area." Sandra bristled and dutifully returned to her preserving pan.

Soon, Bob's little recreational past time had become an obsession and he needed his daily fix of porn to function in this new life. He e-mailed his oldest friend Roger about his favourite occupation and had even listed some web site addresses for him to investigate, but either Roger wasn't interested or considered it all too tacky. Gradually Bob's life diminished, until all he desired to do was be alone with his gyrating ladies on screen. Sandra hadn't a clue about his secret passion. Goodness knows what she would have said if she had known.

Bob received a rather nasty shock when the first telephone bill plopped on to the mat, through their smart brass letterbox. He had spent over three hundred pounds on the Internet clicking on to unsavoury sites. He hid the bill from Sandra, in his old burgundy leather brief case and made a mental note to pay it at the Post Office when out in town.

As Bob became more involved with his diversion he developed into a lonely man who dreadfully missed having his friends around. He then made his fatal mistake. Different women replaced lusty Laura, until Saucy Sadie evolved into Bob's favourite choice. Just peering at her sexy image on his flat screen performing preferred fantasies was everything he lived for now.

Then came the crunch. Sadie wanted to meet him. He was surprised. Although his image was only glimpsed through a web camera, he was flattered she cared enough to want to meet him, being thirty years her senior at least.

The allotted day came; he chose his best brown suit with a cream coloured shirt to wear, a diamond-patterned tie completed his ensemble. He whistled as he prepared for his first date with the lovely Sadie. Just as well he'd received new aftershave for Christmas. He slicked some gooey gel through his sparse grey locks and closed the blue front door, calling out goodbye to Sandra, as he left their home for the final time.

Walking at a brisk pace downhill, towards the town, Bob felt elated. Quickly checking the address again, on a piece of paper in his trouser pocket, he realised Sadie lived in a part of town he had never visited, as it was considered a bit rundown.

Entering a dark forbidding alley Bob felt a small shiver of apprehension run down his spine. This couldn't be the place surely. He hesitatingly knocked at the black wooden door with peeling paint and a rusty handle. The smell of urine pervaded his nostrils.

Bob's fantasy girl Sadie opened the door slowly and pulled him into the narrow unlit corridor. "Come along here Bob and visit my studio where I film everything for your pleasure," she trilled. She was not quite the vision of loveliness he had been expecting. Her black fish net stockings were ripped and her face was similar to a fifty-year-old pair of jeans. His heart began to hammer threateningly in his chest.

Entering Sadie's bedroom the smell of stale sweat and cigarette smoke hit his nostrils and made him gag. "Right Bob I'll keep it short as time is money. You and I can help each other out. My old man rakes in all the cash from the Internet business and gives me nothing to live on. Now that ain't right is it? A girl's got outgoings, hair, makeup and ciggies. So here's what I'll do for you. I'll keep quiet about our little rendezvous if you cough up £100.00 a month for me."

Bob's heart sank. "Sadie, my pension is minimal, that won't leave me any money to live on," he explained.

"That's not my fault, you'll have to pay up else I'll just pop round to yours and tell your missus what you've been up to."

Bob was distraught. "Please Sadie don't do this you'll destroy me. I can't afford it. The phone bill is mounting up as it is. I've hidden it from Sandra but I can't hide any more expenses from her. She's bound to notice something's amiss."

"Not my problem mate I need to get by, you're comfortably off," Sadie airily replied.

As Bob left the stinking ground floor flat, £100.00 worse off, he knew it was no good. He'd have to pay up regularly or risk being exposed to Sandra. He had no option.

Upset, he strode out along the far end of the beach, away from the usual casual strollers. His chest ached he shouldn't have eaten his lunch so quickly but he had been excited at the thought of meeting Sadie in the flesh.

Taking off his brown loafers and argyle socks he wandered into the dunes, feeling the sand crunching between his hairy curled toes. His heart began to pound. He sat down as a massive pain in his chest made him clutch his left breast with an outstretched hand. He fell sideways into the hollow between the dunes lifeless.

A tramp wandering around the dunes later that day found Bob. Realizing he was no more, the vagrant stripped him of his clothes leaving just his blue striped boxer shorts.

The Malingerer

Naomi Stride

'I don't see why we have to leave so soon,'
I complained as we loaded up the car
'She's spoilt our holiday, attention seeking drama queen.'
My husband said nothing.

'Every time we go away she does it,'
I continued as we crossed the Yorkshire Moors.
'She ought to get a life and keep her nose away from ours.'
My husband said nothing.

'She'll have the doctors wrapped around her finger,'
I spat out as we waited for the lift.
'You should tell them she's a whinging hypochondriac.'
My husband said nothing.

'Go and ask them what is wrong with her,'
I demanded as we reached the waiting room.
'I don't expect they'd give us coffee, we've driven fifty miles.'
My husband said nothing.

'So what is wrong with that old bat today?'
I asked when he eventually returned.
'An ingrown toenail, a splinter, perhaps a little cough?'
'She's dead,' he said.

The Sliding Stone

Barbara Calvert

It's nearly the summer holiday. I always think about the sliding stone when it's a holiday. The long holiday is sometimes a bit boring and I just wish we had something like that around here. My grandad used to tell me about his sliding stone when I was little. He came from Ireland and that's where the sliding stone was. It sounded amazing and I always wanted to go there. My grandad said he'd take me one day, but when I was seven he died so we never went. I wish I could have gone to Ireland with him.

My mum was born in England, but her dad, that's my grandad, had come here a long time before that. She didn't know much about the sliding stone. She did go on a visit to Ireland once with her mum and dad, but she didn't go to the sliding stone. She says she was about sixteen, so you can bet she wouldn't have wanted to have a go; afraid of messing up her dress or something. But me, I'd just love a go.

Grandad used to tell me about the village where he lived. It wasn't far from the sea and behind was the mountain. He always called it a mountain, and I always thought that it would be towering over the houses with its top hidden up in the clouds. When the clouds weren't there, you'd see snow on the top. That's what mountains are like. Well, when I was little that's what I thought anything called a mountain would be like. Now I know that mountains around here are not quite like that. I saw a programme on television once about a train that goes up a mountain in Wales, and then people can get off and walk up to the top; ordinary people, wearing ordinary clothes and shoes; not carrying axes and ropes and things like that. We did a project in school and I found out on the internet that Mount Everest is 8,800metres high and the highest mountain in Europe is nearly 5,000.That mountain in Wales, Snowdon, is just over 1,000. So, what I'm saying is that mountains can be quite friendly and easy to climb. The one near my grandad's village was, because him and his mates went up and down all the time and it was mainly because of the sliding stone.

It wasn't actually what you'd call a stone. It was really part of the mountain. It was a sloping bit of the rock; a good, long slope, not too steep, that ended with a nice soft patch of grass. He said there were a few thistles and nettles, but that didn't put them off. Anyway, some time before that; and my grandad said the sliding stone had been going for generations; some time before, some kid must have looked at it and thought

"That would be great to slide down." and his mates probably thought the same. Now, O.K, that doesn't sound too cool. We've got slides in the park, and I've slid off rocks at the beach. In school it's great sliding across the hall floor in your socks, when the caretaker's just polished it for the start of term. But, with lots of sliding, that slope got more and more slippery and shiny. Then someone must have had THE GREAT IDEA! I expect they noticed that there were lots of rocks and boulders about and some daredevil decided to use one of them to sit on and slide down the slope. It must have been great! From then on that's what everyone did. One rule was that you never took the rocks away. They had to stay there for anyone to use. The slope got more and more shiny and so did the sit-on rocks, so the slide down was AMAZING and you finished up in the nice, soft, grassy landing space.

My grandad said all the kids he ever knew went on the sliding stone, and so had his dad and even his grandad. That was what they did in their school holidays; all the time. Can you imagine that? Two hundred years of polishing that rock! They called the sit-on stones, sliders, and I bet some of those sliders have had kids sitting on them who are really old now, and some might even have died years and years ago.

We haven't got any mountains where we live. We've got a park. When I was very little I used to go there with my mum. There's a little playground, mainly for little kids, but not many people use it now. Some of the people round here are trying to get the council to fix it up again because it's a bit wrecked. My mum won't let me go to the park. She says you never know who's hanging about. I think it's not a bad place to play, as long as you don't want to go on the swings and things. There are some good trees for climbing and a couple of little hills covered in bushes. Great for spy games. Me and my mates Chris and Nick have thought up some real good games we could play there, and a few of the others in our class would be up for it too. There's only one small problem; we're not allowed to go there. Well, Nathan Riggs' mum lets him go anywhere, but when I tell my mum that she just says

"Oh that woman would, but you're not going there."
What is it with Nathan's mum? At least she lets him have some fun.

"You never know who's hanging around there." And that's the end of it.

Chris comes home with me some days after school and we play on the computer or watch videos. I told Chris about the sliding stone in Ireland and he thought we might be able to do something like that in the wood up behind school. There wouldn't be any rocky slopes, but there are some grassy banks. If they're not too bumpy it might work. We go there sometimes with Mr Hutton our teacher. It's usually to collect leaves, or measure the circumference of trees or to count the number of flowers in a metre square. We don't get chance to look for good places for sliding, but we might find something there that would do.

I tried to persuade my mum that we needed to go up to the woods for our science homework, but she didn't believe me.

"You're not going there on your own."

"But I wouldn't be on my own. Chris and Nick would be with me," I say.

It's no good. The weirdos in the park apparently hang out in the wood too.

The trouble with my mum is that she watches too much television. She sees all the news, and I know that horrible things do happen to kids, but she watches all those detective programmes too; and those where they have dead bodies stretched out on tables to find out how they died. I think she can't sort out what's real and what's just a story, so she thinks there are thousands of crazy people all over the place.

A few weeks ago Chris came over and we planned a brilliant game for the holidays, like one of my computer games, but this would be for real. It was one of those where you had to search for special objects. We even made some things out of card; a shield, a sword, a treasure chest, things like that. We thought we could hide them around the park, if they won't let us go to the wood. There was a problem though. If we had to hide them ourselves then we'd know where to find them. I did suggest to Chris that perhaps we could ask a couple of the weirdos if they'd hide them for us. I don't think my mum would get the joke.

The things are still under my bed. And, under my bed is my own, secret object too. I found it last year, when we were on holiday. As soon as I saw it I knew it would make a brilliant slider. It was a huge pebble. It was round, about the size of one of my mum's trays. It was flat and smooth and I knew it would be just right for the sliding stone. I could just see myself sitting on it, with my knees bunched up and my heels just about fitting onto the edge. There was just enough thickness in the middle for me to be able to hold on at the edge without crunching my fingers underneath it. I'd make myself comfortable, then, whoosh! I'd be off down that slope that's polished like glass; just like my grandad and his dad too. Then I would climb back up and do it all again, as many times as I wanted.

I know you're not supposed to take stones off the beach, but there were hundreds. They wouldn't have missed just one. I couldn't take it away with me that day, so I hid it until we went back again. I made sure I had my rucksack with me, and it fitted in just right, though it was a bit of a weight. It was really difficult carrying my bag back without anyone noticing how heavy it was!

Every time I look at my slider, I realise that time is running out. I've just got to get them to take me to Ireland before I get too big for it. They've often talked about going there and I know my mum would like to take me to see where my grandad lived. I know exactly how to get to the sliding stone. I think it's absolutely right that, after my grandad and my great-grandad, I should have my turn too. Really, I suppose, my mum ought to have a go as well. That'll take a bit of persuading! Anyway this year it's Florida. I don't think they've got mountains there so, I won't be taking my slider with me, even if I could get it past the check- in at the airport, and I don't think that's likely. But next year? Well maybe. I'll just keep on reminding them. Oh and we'd have to go in the car and on the ferry. I'd never get that stone onto an aeroplane.

Summer

Ann Merrin

JUNE
Month of marriages
Bouquets, bridesmaids: bride blossoms
Groom acquiesces

JULY
Flowers in full bloom
Air filled with pungent perfume
Slow down and enjoy

AUGUST
Watch the tide race in
Watch children race to greet it
Summer seaside bliss

Along The Road To Unicorn Square

Alan Beckett

Realms of wonder dwell gladly in my mind, it's by dreams we live, the woman defined. Right-hand, is the way to kingdoms fair, along the winding road to Unicorn Square.

By numbers we will know, the man replied. Science and logics from the left hand side. Quantification, rule and equation, mathematica, measures and calculation.

No! The right side's the force that will reinforce spiritual dreams, mystical themes of course. Calculation is not the way you see, hope is the child and wonder the mother to be.

Cast out your fairy tales and ghostly thought. It's our left sphere alone that's left to sort, Your guess work, even your best work is not true, unlock your mind; it's so easy to do.

The right side will always be the way to stay, imagination, speculation and creation, I say. I can seek the company of the spirit and of fantasy that our dreams will permit.

Truth is the game; the game is about truth, such is the gift of age to youth. Open your eyes, you are the prize. I care that your far-fetched thoughts blinker your blue sky eyes.

No! You employ such a stumbling wit of quantum physic and binary bit. Truth's your blunt sword; reason your shoes of clay, no wonder you have no wonder, today.

You are indeed a damsel with good fight, pity that such blight should cloud your sight. Objective science and summation to, is the only critical path for me and you.

Look! Try to feel, where there's nothing to touch. See all colour where there's just grey and such. It's a shame and sad when you do so blame. You're shunning the art to worship the frame.

Heh! No matter! The town approaches fast, the symmetry of its fine squares at last. See the one in the centre there. How it calls. I once designed those lines, those noble walls.

Indeed I see and hear the town so near, though you do well to find the square is not just a square. For down there, the people have magic and light. Their lives twixt left and the right, out of sight.

But you must see what majesty there be in that pure form, that trigonometry. Have no fear my dear, the left side will show. It will guide you there and you'll truly know.

They know of maths and extrapolation, and of many Unicorns amidst their nation. For you and me dear, our hands clasped so tight, we are both left and right, such synaptic delight.

Aye, we have known a true contradiction with such opposing views, but together we rejoice in one perception, not to confuse. Our twin spheres, a complementary pair, joined alone along the road to Unicorn Square.

A September Song

Maureen Nicholls

Memory is a fickle jade, providing clear, concise and effortless recall one minute but offering a total blank the next. As we get older, it gets worse. You rush upstairs for something urgently needed, only to gaze manically around with no idea what it was.

I can remember as though it were yesterday, the name of the child I sat next to in class when I first started school aged five; I know the name of the teacher too. But, after a most enjoyable evening spent in the company of our new neighbours, when I wished to thank them for their hospitality, I couldn't for the life of me, remember their names!

Despite such lapses, we are most of us blessed with at least one very special memory; a moment so wonderful, so *memorable*, that every tiny detail is effortlessly and meticulously filed away, never, ever to be forgotten.

I was privileged to have just such a moment one September in 1965, or perhaps it was 1966...oh hell, I don't know, but it was definitely September. My office was opposite the back of the Hippodrome Theatre in Denmark Street. In those days, this area of Bristol was known as 'Little Soho'. A narrow street with a strange mix of buildings; many of the ancient ones had upper floors which leaned perilously towards those opposite, in true Dickensian fashion. Amongst the variety of multi-national restaurants sporting garish neon signs, were offices, pubs, shops and tobacconists, the Railway lost property and, at the far end, possibly the best restaurant in the West Country at that time, Harvey's; discreetly positioned over its own wine cellars dating back several centuries.

A brothel was conveniently situated over one of two nefarious medical appliance shops, the windows of which contained items of such a dubious nature as to cause endless amusement to school children visiting the theatre. Those were the days when 'a packet of three' was something discreetly offered for the weekend by a barber, not commonly displayed with detailed recommendations as to sensitivity and size!

On my journeys to and fro, it was the norm to see lorry's loaded with scenery and props pull up outside the theatre and, as the doors were flung open in readiness, be able to listen to whoever or whatever was being rehearsed on stage. Actors declaiming lines; instruments tuning up; dancer's feet, tapping in time to the shouts of choreographers; singers of every genre practising scales or songs. This was my world, part of my daily existence that I took for granted, as it was for anyone who lived or worked in the vicinity of Denmark Street.

On my *memorable* day, I left the office in a hurry, anxious to be on time for an appointment elsewhere in the city. I hotfooted it up the street only to be brought to a halt by two enormous pantechnicons blocking both road and pavement. I tried to side step the men unloading these monsters into the stage door.

"Oi Miss, get out the way!"

"But I need to get by" I pleaded

"And so you shall, all in good time."

"Please, I'm in a hurry."

Other voices took up the clamour, all of them it seemed, in a hurry.

"Now see what you started," he glared at me. "Get back, go on, the lot of you, get back or so help me I'll drop the bleedin' lot on your toes. Mind your back there missis, for Pete's sake, get out the way."

The men heaved and sweated as they manoeuvred the vast sets between the parked cars and a crowd of impatient bystanders.

A cab driver blew his horn and yelled from his open window, "I've got a fare waiting for me, get out the way."

"Never mind your bloody fare what about my delivery," shouted a van driver, "I can't get me back doors open."

A couple of prostitutes, hanging out of an upper floor window, shrieked with laughter at this last remark. "Come up 'ere darlin', we'll get your back doors open and 'elp you make a real good delivery."

"Filthy tarts!" replied the van driver, but couldn't quite stop a smirk appearing.

As always, in any crowd watching men at work, there was one bloke who thought they were doing it all wrong and kept up a running commentary on how they should go about it. "If you'd only listen to me," he shouted, "I could tell you what to do."

"Why don't you shove your 'ead up your arse and give your gob a rest," came the reply.

"He can't," a wag from the crowd took up the joke, "he's already talking frew is arse."

The road sweeper, who alone seemed unaffected by the uproar, rested on the head of his broom and drew deeply on a woodbine.

Floating clearly over this mayhem could be heard the cacophony that is an orchestra tuning up and the sound of a soprano voice practising scales. For a few moments, the music ceased but when it started again, the opening bars of the orchestra, this time in full and magnificent unison made us all stop in our tracks.

The swelling sound filled the street. Mesmerised I stood absolutely still and listened, as I recognised the introduction to 'Oh my beloved Papa', an aria I knew and loved. I held my breath as a voice from heaven sang the opening words.

'O Mio Babbino Caro'.

Clearly, voluptuously, the glorious voice rose with *'mi piace, e bello.'*

The street noises faded away; all was quiet and still. Every single person stopped what they were doing to listen with ears and hearts to the beautiful music. As the final notes *'Babbo, pieta, pieta'* died away, a pin dropped at the top of the street would have been clearly heard by those at the bottom.

For what seemed like an age, there was complete and utter silence. Then, the whole street erupted in an ovation the singer would have loved. We clapped and cheered, 'bravo' and 'encore'. Drivers hung from car windows, yelling and blowing their horns; the cook from the café banged his saucepan lids and one of the prostitutes threw a toilet roll from her window, hanging on to the end, waving and shouting as it blew like a pink banner above the heads of those below.

Everyone was asking, "who is it? Who? WHO IS IT?"

The street cleaner turned towards me, tears streaming down his face. "Ignorant pigs, it's La Stupenda!"

I could hardly see him for the tears in my own eyes and I repeated "La Stupenda? Do you mean Joan Sutherland?"

"Course I bloody do! Who else can sing like that?" He wiped his face, threw his brush into the cart and carried on his way up the street.

My appointment forgotten, I rushed round to the box office. I must get tickets, please let there be tickets. Sadly, there were none. The sublime, Aussie was in Bristol for just one night; all seats had sold out months ago.

During the intervening years, I've been lucky enough to attend countless operas in many towns and city's both at home and abroad; I've enjoyed some wonderful

"It's all my fault. It's my fault that Timmy's over there. It's my fault that everyone is leaving." She spoke calmly as if stating indisputable facts. He had heard these words many times before; often in anguish; sometimes in anger; but today they were free of any emotion. The past months had moved them all to this point of inevitability, and yet she still took the burden of blame upon herself.

"Maggie my love, it's not your fault. It isn't anyone's fault. Timmy was ill. None of us realised just how ill he was."

"But I should have known. I was his mother. If we'd taken him across in the morning, he might still be here now."

"He might, but he might not. We'll never know for sure."

It had started as a tummy pain that had got worse as the day went on, and as the storm outside had grown stronger. Then it was too late. It had become impossible to get the boat out to cross over to the mainland; so near yet unreachable.

When it was all over, it was obvious to everyone that their time on the island was coming to an end. With Timmy gone there was not a single child left, and most of the adults of Maggie and Sam's generation had left years before. To the mainland, and even further away to America they had gone; to seek new, more comfortable lives with opportunities the island could never give them. The older folk knew that in all likelihood, there would soon be no one left to support them. The fish and the few vegetables they took across to the markets were becoming less important to the mainlanders. Their island life was becoming part of history. So plans had been made for a different future, and this was the first day of that new beginning.

Maggie had just one more thing to do.

"I just have to pick some heather for Timmy's flowers." It was time to go. With his arm around her shoulders Sam led Maggie down the cliff path for the last time.

One Saturday Afternoon
on
Clevedon Station

Alan Beckett

I held the print between forgetting fingers,
Had it just been raining? Who remembers?
What was it really like, so long ago on that wet afternoon?
After all, a photo is just patches of light modulated by form.

The platform stretched into the greenness of Somerset's light.
The distant roof of the engine shed sparkled, fresh and bright.
A small engine with a single carriage, sulphurous and smelly.
But there is no one. No one there to feel the fire in its belly.

No one to hear the popping valves and gentle hissing,
No one else there on that day. She was missing.
Just a tantalising snapshot. A two dimensional history.
A passing moment captured in a picture. A mystery.

I waited there for her. We were to elope.
The Kodak had just snapped at empty space, void of hope.
Frozen for all that time. I recall and shiver,
For she and the little station, have now gone forever.

The Round Dozen

Ann Merrin

"One day it'll be my turn," murmured Julia quietly. She turned her back on the crowds and walked across the square with her head held high, as if rehearsing the great day.

She returned to her present employment and was greeted by the screeching voice of Miss Wilberforce, to whom she was companion.

"I've been sitting here all morning – on my own. Not a soul to talk to. I haven't had a cup of tea since seven o'clock. Where have you been?"

"I went to post your letter. Just as you ordered. And now I shall make you a cup of tea."

Julia moved quietly to the kitchen and began her preparations for tea-making. She was a slight figure, with a small, disappointed face. At the age of thirty-five there was no prospect of marriage for her, nor any opportunity of making a social life for herself. She had devoted her life to caring for elderly persons after the death of her own grandmother fifteen years ago. It sometimes seemed to her that her whole life had been a battle against the tyranny of old age. There came a time in life when people felt they had a right to say what they pleased, regardless of anyone else's feeling. And it always seemed to be Julia's feelings that were disregarded.

She returned to the sitting room with the tea tray neatly laid and poured tea for Miss Wilberforce in her fine, bone-china cup.

"Oh, for goodness sake! This tastes like cat's pee! What on earth have you put in it – are you trying to poison me?"

"It probably tastes different because of the sweetener the doctor told us to use instead of sugar. I'd have thought you were so thirsty, you would be glad of any drink."

"Well, I'm not. I'll finish this cup but you can just go and make another pot of tea, and bring my real bloody sugar!"

And so the day carried on as it had done for six months now: Miss Wilberforce commanding and complaining; Miss Julia moving quietly and efficiently about her. It seemed to be taking much longer this time. Probably something to do with Miss Wilberforce's great bulk – she was at least three stone overweight. Julia could wait.

Over the last fifteen years Julia had poisoned twelve of her employers. Quietly and efficiently. She had started with her own grandmother. She had been sure she would be caught. Having succeeded once, twice, then three times, it became a sort of hobby. Choosing the employer; allowing them to express the foulest side of their nature; watching their health deteriorate; sometimes rapidly, sometimes slowly. That was Julia's choice. She would always choose the chemist carefully – never the same one twice in a row. Yes, it was a hobby in which Julia took a pride, though she knew one day it might be the death of her.

Miss Wilberforce eventually died, and Julia was left to arrange the funeral. In a small area like Hampstead there were at least five reputable undertakers; Julia used them in rotation. Unfortunately for her, one of the young pall-bearers had taken to her sad, slight figure standing at the lonely graveside and, seeing her on this third occasion, felt moved to speak to her.

"Another lost relative?"

"No. No, actually it was my employer."

In the split second of that first 'No', their eyes met and Julia felt a thrill of fear run through her. The young man, for his part, had not seen at all what he had expected in the eyes of the small, quiet female to whom he had been attracted. He saw the fear, and he also saw a cold glitter in those eyes, framed by a hard, lined face. They drew apart and went their separate ways.

Back at the undertaker's, a discussion took place about the strange young lady at today's funeral. Mr Black, the head mortician said he too had seen the lady before, and not when he was working here, but over at Turnbull's, in West Hampstead.

"Quite a regular angel of death, if you ask me!"

"You might well have hit the nail on the head, Mr Black," said John thoughtfully.

So, this person had been at four funerals at least in the last five years while he had been working here. Oh, the chaps laughed at his amateur sleuthing, but this time he had seen the eyes and he was sure he was on to something. He could check the name on their records. Then it should be easy enough to find out from the other local undertakers whether funeral arrangements had been made with them by this same person.

Twelve. TWELVE. There had been twelve funerals. And now the living manifestation of those dead faced Julia from the jury box. Once John had checked out his suspicions, the police had worked swiftly in gathering all the information they needed to condemn Miss Julia Stern. She stood, small, silent, resolute, as she listened to the judge decree that she "be hanged by the neck until dead."

"I knew my turn would come," murmured Julia quietly, and she held her head high while the crowds in the square shouted and jeered, just as they had that day not so very long ago.

Sleep Solution

Patricia Welford

Its 2 am, although I try, I cannot sleep
Mountainous burdens grown from a mole heap
Trying hard to right the wrongs of society
Whatever shall I do to stop all the anxiety?

I must try to use my imagination
The wrongs and tribulations of our nation
Little me alone, my worry cannot right
So I lie down again and put out the light

In my mind I get out a large heavy box
I fasten it up tight and close with strong locks
All the tribulations, I have put within
Trouble free, my fantasies can now begin

I am soon outside on a beautiful day
The sun is high and hot as I find my way
Sky azure blue, wind so light it calms my soul
Looking around, I make straight for my goal

There it is, my wonderful tropical beach
Waves gently break, white horses within reach
Caressing my ankles so gentle a beat
Relishing, soft white sand beneath my feet

I continue paddling idly though warm water
Jumping, I ripple with joyous laughter
Splashing, childlike with pure innocent delight
Entranced by the vision, my beach in the night

There I linger contented, just me alone
For experience before to me has shown
As I move from the shallows into the deep
Silently, drowsily, I have gone to sleep

The Pirates of Trevone

Naomi Stride

Near the Cornish town of Padstow
Lies the inlet of Trevone
A place that many years ago
Some pirates called their home.

In caves concealed midst dog-tooth rocks
The pirates stashed their loot
They cared not what their victims lost
Those men of disrepute.

The men of Padstow were incensed,
The pirates were too near,
Their wives and daughters were not safe,
They lived their lives in fear.

An aging Priest had seen enough,
He had to make a stand,
Speaking in a local tavern,
He told them of a plan.

"Men of Padstow we must unite,
and stop these buccaneers.
Our God will Bless the men who stand
As willing volunteers."

And so that night a few brave men,
Set out towards Trevone,
United by a common foe,
They would protect their homes.

They saw the pirates landing boat,
Pushed high up on the sand,
They knew this was their chance and charged,
Their weapons in their hands.

The pirates, although caught off guard,
Were well equipped to fight
They fought without the fear of death
And battled through the night.

The pirates lost that bloody fight
The villagers were free
But haunted by the ghosts of men
Whose lives were on the sea

Now whispers surfing off-shore winds
Mix with thunderous waves
Warning all who walk these shores
They stand on pirate's graves.

A Perfect Day

Patricia Welford

Early morn I from my window looked
The sun was up, a full spring day
The grass with dew sparkling touched
The bluebells in gentle wind did sway

This is my favourite time of year
Delighted to spend my one free day
Amongst the bluebells I hold so dear
To sit awhile, idle my time away

The scent o'powering the senses reeling
Happy memories come back to mind
Of other years amongst my wood a sitting
A greater pleasure I doubt I'll find

The Boto Man

Maureen Nicholls

The lake was not really a lake at all but an inland tributary of the mighty Amazon. Century's ago, the deep chocolate brown river had discovered a tiny crack between the high red rocks, separating the river from the rain forest and had seeped slowly, inexorably through the gap. Over time, it flooded the deep basin of soft sandy loam and created a mysterious hidden playground for river creatures of every kind.

Tatiané had disobeyed her father. Never before had she done such a thing and her pulses raced. She found the spot she was seeking; it was at the end of a fallen tree, where the bark was smooth and round; a seat on which to sit and let her feet and legs dangle in the water. The air temperature was cooler now but the water still felt warm and inviting. The moon hung low in the sky and its reflected light shone like a path over the glassy surface, touching the girls face, giving it an ethereal beauty.

He would come back. Even her mother agreed this was so.

"Boto men will always return until they get what they want," she had said.

"Boto men?" Her father was angry. "You stupid woman, there is no such thing. Boto are Inia's, the pink river dolphins. They do not suddenly become men. How can you believe such stupid stories?"

Creola eyed her husband calmly. "Have you forgotten Teodoro so quickly, Joaquim?"

Joaquim returned his wife's steady gaze and his mouth tightened to a thin line. "I do not forget," he said and walked hurriedly away from the two women.

Tatiané immediately begged her mother to tell all about her aunt Teodoro but her mother's only response was a sad shake of the head as she bent to continue her work in the manioc field.

Tatiané didn't care anymore. If he really was a Boto Man, so be it. She wanted him; wanted to feel the strength of his beautiful body; to touch him as his arms held her and his lips and voice caressed her.

The first night he came it had been so hot. She had moved her hammock to the trees below the house where she could feel a light breeze. Almost asleep she became aware of him standing next to her. Tall and slim, dressed in a beautiful white suit with a hat pulled down, hiding his eyes. He took her hand in his. He was irresistible, compelling, like no man she had ever known.

"Come dance with me," his voice was soft and low.

She stood. "We have no music," she laughed.

"We have music in our souls," he said and took her into his arms. Their bodies swayed as one; languorous movements that filled her with an ecstasy she had never known before. He lifted her into his arms and carried her as he would a child, to the water's edge. In the shallows, in the darkness, they were one and she was filled with a passion known only by the fortunate few.

Each night he came, each night they danced and made love and then sat, where she was sitting now, talking and watching the moon before it was time for him to leave. She never saw him go, just as she never saw him arrive but suddenly he was there and suddenly, he was gone.

All night she waited and the next night and the next. Months passed and still she called to him, every evening when the moon was low over the water, but he never returned.

***

The tiny infant lay beside her in the hammock. Her mother came with a little hat for the baby to wear.

"Deolinda doesn't need that," Tatiané laughed and pushed the hat away.

"Yes she does my daughter. We must hide the tiny blow hole, the mark of the Boto, or everyone will know". Creola pulled the soft white cotton over the baby's head. Then she sighed. "Not that they don't know already. I wonder how long we will be able to keep her?"

Tatiané stared at her mother's stoical face. The stories about Boto babies were the nursery rhymes of the Amazona's. Girls were always warned that if they allowed a Boto man to make love to them, one day he would return for the baby. Tatiané knew it was so and had planned that when her lovely man returned he could take his child, but she intended to make him take her too. She smiled and touched the top of the little white hat.

Creola knew that smile and remembered her sister Teodoro. There was nothing to be done and she turned away to hide her tears.

The Gift
Patricia Lloyd

It came unexpectedly this wondrous gift
Across the dinner table – placed on my mat.
A dear friend thought, it was "right" for me
And by doing so gave great pleasure.

I had not expected that dark cold night
That I would be feted in such a way
That I would receive a gift so great
A gift I would treasure, for ever.

A book? A very old book –
Worn black leather (but still well bound)
Lettering in gold still clear to see
Showed six letters, they spelt "MILTON".

My hand lifted the front cover –
Anticipation, awaited the learning
For I did not know much of Milton –
Anxious to read and find out!

"The Poetical Works of John Milton" I read
"With Memoir, Explanation Notes etc."
Disbelief and reticence made me ask
"Is this really for me"? – to have it confirmed
Lovingly, – "Definitely."

The book sits near at hand so that I can explore
First the memoir to find the man, and after
that, maybe "Paradise Lost" or will it be
"Paradise Regained".
Wonder!

Take Off

Alan Beckett

Receiving clearance from the control tower and despite the worsening blizzard, the old pilot eased back on the stick and the heavily laden aircraft slid majestically along the snow-covered runway.

Once air-born behind the line of reindeer stretching ahead, the red-cloaked pilot chuckled. "Here we go again."

Winter

Ann Merrin

DECEMBER

Advent leads to light

Winter's fete is upon us

Cheer in cheerless days!

JANUARY
Short, cold wintry days

Let it snow, let the wind blow

Read a book dear friend

FEBRUARY

More snow, more dark days

Do you see a chink of light?

Sunshine on snowdrops

Ten More Minutes

Naomi Stride

Sitting with her back against the trunk of a majestic old oak she gazed up at the changing leaves and wondered whether she had, in fact, left the oven on. She could remember shutting the windows, locking and bolting the back door, closing the bedroom doors and switching off every electrical appliance in the house, but she could not, for the life of her, remember switching off the oven. She closed her eyes and tried to visualise her last moments in the house, but the overriding memory had been her husband honking the horn and shouting at her to get a move on, everyone was waiting. He had no patience with her compulsion to safeguard their home before she left. She knew he found the routine annoying, but despite her best efforts, her nature forbade her to leave her home vulnerable.

She glanced over to where her husband lay sprawled, practically comatose, beer bottle in hand and flabby stomach protruding between his charity shop trousers and ban the poll-tax T-shirt. A fly was picking its way through the exposed forest of fuzz, and the sun was gently reflecting off the bald patch he insisted was her imagination. She considered disturbing his slumber by asking if he had turned the oven off, but knew his answer would only reflect what he knew she wanted to hear, whether it be truthful or not.

Remnants of the picnic lay scattered over the patched brown rug, crisp crumbs swirling in a spilled drink and crusts from mauled sandwiches already curling in the afternoon sun. The locusts that had devoured the meal were now playing in a shallow stream, armed with nets and buckets, peering intently at the trickling water, hoping to catch something wriggly and slimy.   She smiled as she listened to their shrill voices arguing.   They were always arguing.   She had given up trying to sort out their numerous quarrels.   She had come to the conclusion that arguing with your brothers and sisters was part of growing up, and although she would intervene should it come to blows, if it was just vocal, she let them get on with it.

A loud snore disturbed her thoughts and she began to feel slightly disgruntled.   Why was it always down to her to watch the children?   Why couldn't she lie back and have a snooze whilst he took charge?   But she knew why.   Her husband didn't seem to have the same sense of danger as she did, couldn't foresee accidents in the same way.   He was a good father and loved his children dearly, but whilst he was good at picking up the pieces after an accident, she could usually prevent them happening, and that meant that she would always be the most appropriate carer.

She had embraced it as her role.   Since the first time she held her eldest child in her arms she had abandoned herself to its tiny being.   When children two and three came along she divided her time as equally as she could between them, her husband and her home.   Juggling nappies, feeding and tantrums with the cooking and cleaning she learned to take satisfaction in the most menial accomplishments.   The day that she had managed to vacuum the stairs from top to bottom as well as keeping up with the breastfeeding demands of a hungry baby seemed miraculous, until her husband came home and grumbled that there was still wet laundry in the machine.   At least it got into the bloody machine, she had thought, but had said nothing.

Babyhood and toddler life had not lasted long enough despite the fact she had nurtured three children through it.   Now they were older, and all at school, they were quickly growing away from her.   They no longer searched for her breast when they were hungry, grizzled for her attention when they needed changing, or fell asleep in her arms after an exhausting morning. She was far from redundant, but their increasing independence had come quicker than she wanted. She was not ready to let go, not quite yet.

She had turned the oven off! She smiled as she suddenly had a flashback of turning the knob to zero and realising that it had felt rather sticky. She had made a mental note to clean it on Monday, but she had quite definitely turned the oven off. She was still in control.

Oh yes, she was very much in control and not yet ready to let go. She wanted another baby, but her husband had insisted that three children were enough. Her body had ached with the emptiness of longing, desperate to feel one last time a tiny being growing inside her. She allowed herself a secret smile as she placed her hand flat against her stomach. Soon she would feel it again. Her husband could never predict accidents and he had certainly not predicted this one.

The wind suddenly changed direction and she shivered slightly as the apple tree waved to a new rhythm. She noticed for the first time that it was covered in tiny apple buds, a promise of an abundant harvest. She looked at the watch on her husband's wrist, ten more minutes she promised herself and then she would tell him. Ten more minutes before she called the children back from the stream; ten more minutes before they headed back to their suburban semi; ten more minutes before she had to share her secret. Just ten more minutes.

Sunset Rising

Alan Beckett

Eyes, hands, fingers, wood, earth, waves, wind, rope, sails, ship, berth, light, amber, sunburn, sunset, pall, church, basement, shadows, garden, wall.

Evening, mist, shade, mirror, glass, sunset, shadows, grass, weeds, branches, ivy, trees, trunks, autumn, shadows, leaves.

Air, cold, damp, slime, snails, eyes, hands, fingernails, fangs, lips, blood, bile, girl, neck, smile.

Sure Retribution

Jane Mason

Soon the storms swept eastwards, the sky cleared and the sun beat brutally down on the little house by the cove; and after three sweaty uncomfortable days, the stench from the garage became unbearable.

Carefully, slowly pushing his way out of a mass of dead bodies Juan hauled his thin legs behind his torso, away from the weight of death. He avoided looking at the macabre sight, still in shock, trying instead to focus on his escape.

He could hear the soldiers in the house laughing and drinking, unashamed of their recent massacre. What had happened was sickening, but to them it was all in a days work. Evil bandits they were, enjoying wreaking their form of misery.

Now free of the mass Juan inched along to the window, holding his nose as he did so, the smell of stinking rotting flesh pervading his nostrils if he didn't. Accidentally knocking over a chair in his nervous state, he held his breath to see if they would hear it.

Luckily they were too busy; playing with their painted half dressed whores, to notice anything was amiss. Lifting his dark head to the window Juan peered out. He quickly ducked back down again after spotting one of the soldiers relieving himself against the back of the old house. Counting to sixty, with his brown eyes tightly shut, he looked out again, thankful the soldier had gone and the yard was clear.

He had to make a run for it that was his only way out, no one would think a corpse could escape. They were too busy pleasuring themselves. Quietly opening the weather-beaten door, sounds of lapping waves far below on the shore reached his extra sensitive ears and he sidled around the back of the garage. His heart hammered so terrifyingly in his chest he felt sure they must be able to hear it.

Running to the steps he lowered himself to the sandy shore and relative safety. Luckily the boat was still tied up at the back of the beach and as stealthily as he could he pulled it to the waters edge and into the surf. Clambering into the vessel he rowed out to sea, away from his enemies and certain death.

Juan pulled the oars, as he never had, if they spotted him he would be shot at, perhaps killed. It was worth the risk to put distance between him and the horrible scene on the cliff top. His whole family mowed down before his eyes, their screams reverberating through the night, no mercy being shown by the soldiers to women and children.

He'd been hidden beneath his Mothers skirt. She had protected and saved him. Now it was his turn to seek revenge and justice for the twenty people murdered in cold blood behind the house.

Rowing back to shore a lone fisherman spotted him and ran to assist with the boat. Juan acted as though he'd been out for a pleasure trip, instead of trying to save his life.

"Don't you know it's dangerous around here since the coup, get home before dusk and the curfew to be safe," he warned. Juan just nodded obediently before running away from the beach into town.

Out of breath he arrived at the front of the soldiers barracks in the deserted town square. If he couldn't beat them he would join them. He had fervently read 'Leadership Secrets of Attila the Hun' so revenge would be that much easier with his attained knowledge. He could also learn everything he needed to know about the perpetrators of the heinous crime, so recently committed, from Army soldiers.

Time did not dissuade Juan's purpose in life. He would make those bastards pay for their atrocious actions. All he needed was to be trusted within the ranks and then wait for his moment of reprisal. It didn't matter how many years he had to defer action; his tenacity would be his strength.

Juan signaled to his driver he was ready to go and the Army jeep pulled away in a cloud of dust. As he stepped down from the vehicle he brushed off his epaulettes with his hands and straightened his army uniform ready to meet the General. It had been five years since the overthrowing of the old government and Juan had diligently worked his way up the ranks to senior officer status. He had requested a private meeting with the General to discuss peacekeeping tactics.

He felt his left breast pocket with his right hand for what felt like the hundredth time that afternoon. It contained papers extensively detailing the crime against his people, together with names of the men involved. Juan's jaw jutted out with determination as he marched into the Generals house.

The soldier on the door saluted Juan and held it open for him to pass into the air-conditioned interior. The opulent furnishings were foreign to him; far surpassing the basic accommodation other officers were afforded. This was obviously the reward for having the audacity to overthrow your ruling government.

In the outer sanctum another officer checked Juan's credentials and escorted him into the General. Then and only then did Juan realise the mistake he had made in coming here, for standing to the right of the General was the man who had ordered the atrocity. Juan fingered the handgun beneath his jacket wondering.

Street Feet

Alan Beckett

If you have a moment to care and stare at an old bod who trundles askew across the frozen dew. If you have a moment I would like you to meet my feet.

They are not what one might observe as being neat feet, nor are they by any expression of compression, flat feet; although they are sometimes by necessity, fleet feet. They are my street feet.

In my game, with much shame to blame you cannot beat good street feet. They part you from hubble bubble, old bill and yobbo. Flat, built for speed, not to bleed, not to impede your parting. It can be such sweet sorrow when one should need to borrow a fellow's dry foot attire sneaked from the flickering shadows of a smoky fire. It is then that you need fleet, street feet. Left and a right, no need to stay in sight; no need to fight; not too bright.

I have street feet to bounce my mentholated, marinated, blobby body along a million miles of pavements, blind alleys, deaf doorways and lowered eyes that despise us shuffling by.

My street feet keep me heart moving. They are not pansy, sweet smelling, neat, elite feet, but feet that have seen and been everywhere, done this, done that, bought the tee-shirt feet.

If you have a moment I would like you to meet my feet. They are my beat feet and I have to go everywhere they know. They are the boss. I don't have any say so, where they go, I go, you see.

"Ere mate, would you like to buy a 'Big Issue'? Me feet are aching something chronic, I think they are in need of a tonic. Oh! You don't have any change. Now feet, there's strange."

The Flower Show

Barbara Calvert

Pat
The tea urn is full
and the cups are set out.
I really don't know
what the fuss is about.

Sylvia
We've plenty of biscuits
and piles of cakes,
And the Devon cream teas
are set out on the plates.

Pat
It didn't take long,
and we're ready to go,
I'm sure we're in for
a really good show.
Now all we can do
is stand here and wait.

Sylvia
Oh where are those judges?
I hope they're not late.
Have you seen that hydrangea?
It looks quite moth-eaten.
There's no doubt, this year,
they're sure to be beaten.

Pat
That arrangement of fuchsias
looks a bit sad,

My Michael's are better.
I bet he feels glad
that Mr O'Donegal passed on this year.
He was always the one
that Mike had to fear.

Sylvia   D'you see those tomatoes?
They're too good to be true.
That Muriel Grimshaw,
 she knows what to do.
I saw her in Waitrose
just two days ago.
She spent quite some time
by the salads you know.

Pat   I think there are others
who've done just the same.
It's really not fair
when they don't play the game.
The jams and the cakes
are looking quite good.
I'd liked to have entered if only I could.
But I haven't had time to pick all the fruit
And my Victoria sponge
got squashed in the boot.

Sylvia   Look, here come the judges,
they're ready to start.
Good luck with your marrow…….

Pat   ………….And with your apple tart.

Lunar Waves

Alan Beckett

We are often told by our astronomers so bold that our Moon moves our seas with comparative ease. I would love to know and perhaps you can show why when the Moon is so light and small and under Earths superior gravitational pull, why its dust does not rise, swell and flow upon some undiscovered lunar beach.

If I speculate onwards and I turn this fanciful idea Moonwards, imagine if you will on a summers day, calm and still, waves of dust surging towards a rocky shore with little Lunar swimmers splashing in a powdery sea called Tranquillity.

Leap Year Gate

Patricia Welford

I stepped outside. The cold midnight air was filled with a frosty mist. Restless and sighing I made my way across the yard to the stables. As I switched on the light, I touched the sign above the door, tracing my fingers over Edwin Quest and Son Limited. It was a habit I had grown into, a small comfort, a link with the past. My father had added the Son to the firms name on my 21st birthday ten years before.

Today is 29th February 2004 and exactly four years ago my widowed father Edwin Quest senior, had mysteriously disappeared riding his favourite mare Sphere. Why he had taken her out in the middle of the February night, neither I nor the police could fathom.

Losing my mother earlier that year to cancer had been a terrible blow, then father disappearing, sent me into a dreadful despair.

During the first few months I became a recluse. I slowly managed to pull myself around, by spending all my spare time from the farm schooling my Arabian colt Orion, who was my only solace during those dark days.

Now four years on the pain had receded. I had the farm work under control and I was beginning to re-enter the social life of the small village, helped by a wonderful young woman I had met at the bank. Thinking of Emily, I felt immediately better; she would soon be my wife. Warmed by my thoughts of her and the wedding to come I walked over to the stables, going in quickly to keep the heat in. The sweet smell of hay and horse assailed my nostrils and I breathed it in deeply as I moved over to the loose boxes.

Orion whinnied a greeting, turning around from his hay net, tossing his noble head before stretching over the half door for a fuss.

'Hello boy, you're lucky it's nice and warm in here, I shall soon be buying you a stable mate ready for Emily.' I told him. He nuzzled my hand, his warm breath caressing my skin. I patted his neck and tickled his chin. Orion, now a full grown stallion looked magnificent, his chestnut coat gleamed with health. His temper was, as many stallions, fickle, untrustworthy with other people, but he knew I knew all his whiles and the loving trust we had between us was unique.

Just then a blast of cold air gusted through as the door was opened. I tried to turn, alarm quickening my heartbeat, but I found myself falling to the ground with strong arms binding me.

'I mean you no harm, I'll let up if you up if you listen to me,' a strong voice spoke into my ear.

'OK, OK, who are you? What do you want? What are you doing here?' my words tumbled out surprise turning into anger.

'I've come from your father,' the voice went on; 'will you listen?'

'My father is dead,' I answered as I attempted to rise. He released me slowly.

Scrambling to my feet I saw my assailant for the first time. The young man smiled apologetically. He was dressed strangely in a brown tunic and leggings with soft leather moccasins.

'My name is Trian,' he said as he delved into his pocket and pulled out a ring. 'Your father said I should give you this.'

'Where did you get that?' my voice became harsh, steeled with anger. I glared at him. 'This is my father's ring.'

'He is well, he came through the gate, to my land Ardenia,' the stranger explained. 'He gave me his ring so you would believe me but we have little time, he is waiting, we must go quickly, saddle your horse, he is needed,' he urged.

I stared at him in rage and astonishment, 'You barge into my stable, holding my dead father's ring, and expect me to take a valuable horse out in the middle of the night on your say so!' I stormed. 'I don't think so, I'm ringing the police,' I took out my mobile and started to punch numbers.

'Wait, think it over,' he pleaded. 'When he gave me the ring, he told me your mother's maiden name. How would I know that?'

I don't know why I believed him, whether it was his anxious tone, his honest face or his alien clothes. Would a thief, or worse, a murderer come dressed up in a pantomime costume? Baffled I shook my head trying to clear the confusion.

The phone was still active in my hand. I closed it down. We stood looking at each other, breathing heavily, weighing each other up, neither of us saying anything.

He spoke first begging. 'Please believe me. Your mothers name was Swann, and your father has named his new homelands after her it is called Swanndell. He and the land need you to bring Orion, and quickly, there is little time, I will explain on the way. My name is Trian, he repeated, 'which means in our world, horse keeper. We are responsible for the welfare and protection of our Arab herd.' He dipped his head, but not before I saw his eyes were filled with anguish at some unspoken pain. 'May I speak to your horse?' he asked.

I nodded acceptance. Moving over to the loose box, Trian spoke softly whispered words. Orion bent his magnificent neck, lowering his head to Trian his ears forward listening he nuzzled gently into his hand.

Orion convinced me, he was calm. Normally nervous and skittish in the presence of people he seemed unfazed by this unknown man. 'OK you win, if Orion accepts you we'll go.' I found myself saying, hardly believing my own ears.

Trian had Orion saddled and reined with the smooth professionalism of an experienced horseman, immediately winning my respect.

'All ready to go?' he enquired.

'What about you? Do you have a mount?' I queried.

'Oh yes I have Elsa outside,'Trian replied. He led Orion out of the stables.

Closing the door I saw Elsa for the first time, untethered waiting patiently for her rider to return. As Trian handed over Orion's reins to me the stable lights showed Elsa as a strongly built roan, reminiscent of a dales pony. She had a neat head surrounded by an abundant mane.

Trian leapt upon her bareback and immediately she trotted off leaving Orion and I to follow on. We left the courtyard, turning down the bridle path alongside the farm entrance. The mist became thicker as we descended down into the gullied path. It clung to our clothes damply. There was no moonlight and I wondered how we could continue, but Trian and Elsa plodded on, Orion and I following in blind faith.

'How about that explanation?' I called to Trian as the horses slowed to a walk over the softer ground.

'Not now,' he exclaimed. 'Wait until the mist clears.'

We proceeded, the mist getting thicker until it seemed to form huge grey globules out of itself, which seemed to congeal and then turn into water soaking our clothes further.

Orion's ears were beginning to flatten and he started prancing about, unhappy about the dark wet atmosphere and his footing. I felt his fear travel from his withers and back up through my legs, but the mare carried on steadily and as the path was narrow, Orion couldn't turn around or push past her. Trian, realising Orion's fear, muttered a few words quietening him immediately.

'Thanks for that Trian,' I said impressed. 'He was beginning to panic.'

'He'll follow Elsa don't you worry,' Trian replied confidently.

As he spoke the thickened mist was starting to change into torrential rain, but some kind of invisible shield domed around our little party, keeping us from any further drenching. As we passed through, it became clearer and clearer until it was transparent, crystal like in the dawn, which had crept up unnoticed in the mist.

An aurora of light shone brilliantly around the shield which held back the cascading water. On either side of us a mirage of colours, reflecting, sparkling, dancing, rainbow like, from torrent to torrent. The noise was now tremendous, the roar of water pouring from a great height, crashing down on either side of our path, the horses hoofs striking unheard the solid rock beneath them.

We are inside a waterfall! I realised in amazement. The noise was too great to speak. Orion and I were led on, until suddenly we were the other side.

Leaving the water behind us, riding into the early morning warmth of a bright summer's day, we came onto a grassy slope. Trian reined in Elsa, and turning back in his saddle his young body stiffened with pride.

'Welcome to the valley of Ardenia. Isn't it wonderful?' he said fervently.

I looked around. Behind us the waterfall fell from some 20 ft above down into fast moving rapids, wide and furious at this point, tumbling again no doubt within a short distance. Lush grassy banks, spring flowers showing up between the blades, white, rose and blue, distant hills marking the valleys edges lined with conifers, reminded me of home.

The air was soft with a tranquil breeze lifting the horses' manes. We went on climbing the immediate bank and levelling out along a track.

Trian started to explain. 'I will let your father tell you what happened to him,' he began, 'I will explain about how I came and why.'

We were riding abreast so I just nodded my assent, not wanting to stop his flow.

'Many hundreds of years ago our ancestors, a group of travelling players, stumbled through the gate. Quite how it happened has been lost in time. Perhaps they never knew!' He paused for a moment. 'Their most treasured possessions were four Arabian horses,' he continued. 'Three mares and a stallion, a fiery creature so the legend goes, only controllable by his owner Trian.'

He looked towards me smiling, reading my look. 'Yes I am a direct descendant, there must always be Trian the horse keeper, just as there must always be Arabian Horses, or the land will fail.' He stopped, busy with his thoughts. I let the silence between us lengthen sensing that Trian would continue in his own time.

The morning air was invigorating. The bird song charmed our ears, and the horses' hooves thudded softly upon the grass.

'This land is so beautiful,' Trian murmured, 'my ancestors did not want to leave it. Everything was here for them and they settled, all but one young man who volunteered to return through the gate to guard its secret. And all our people and horses are descended from that time.'

'Elsa is not an Arab,' I interrupted.

'No. The ponies populated the land before our clan's time. They are sturdy and can pull our carts and help us in the fields. They are like gold and are well valued.' He said affectionately.

'But the people believe that the magic of the gate only holds while we have the Arabs and they are considered sacred, they are never ridden or tamed, they roam free in the Ardenia valley.

But you've missed the point about the man who returned. His name was Edwin Quest your ancestor. No one knows the mystery of the Gate or why it exists, but he had to wait exactly 4 years until the next February 29th for the gate to reopen.

Legend demands of us that whenever the lands need is great, Trian must go back as soon as possible to fetch Edwin Quest to help us.' He put his hand on my arm. 'It is our fate.' he said looking at me reflectively.

I returned his gaze considering. 'It is a fact through the generations of Quests the eldest son is called Edwin, and the family have always lived at the farm and reared Arabs.'

'We are here.' Trian interjected.

As we rounded the bend a cottage appeared in the near distance. Outside a man was chopping logs and stacking them to dry. A lump came into my throat. How many times had I seen that action with the axe I knew without doubt that the man I now looked at was my father.

I spurred Orion on to a gallop and pulling him up a moment or two later I looked down on the man I thought had been killed four years before. The emotions chased through me, exultant triumph to find him at last won out over anger and frustration of the unnecessary grief I had been made to endure. 'Dad! God! Dad! You're alive!' was all I managed to blurt out.

After we had hugged each other again and again and finished clapping each other on the back, we stepped away and inspected each other.

'You look just the same,' we both said together and laughter finally broke the tension.

'Welcome to Swanndell Edwin, do you like my new home?' My father swept his arms wide, contentment showing on his bearded face.' He led me to a small wooden table with chairs spaced around it. 'Sit you must be tired after that journey.'

'Why didn't you come back Dad?' I couldn't help myself asking frankly, 'do you realise the worry and grief I've been through?'

'The Land has been at War, Edwin, I was called to help, but as I emerged along the river valley an arrow found me.' He bent down to show me a scar just above the right knee. 'I was too ill to travel back and today is the first gateway since then.'

'You can return with me,' I said enthusiastically standing up. 'Let's not waste any time the gate may close.'

My father rushed up from his chair crashing it back, a fierce look upon his face. 'No Edwin that is not possible,' he said sternly. 'The war is barely over, and peace was declared only two months ago. I cannot leave, as there is much to be done. The people are in despair. The land beyond this valley has been ravaged by the war and they are almost without hope. One of the last battles set alight the great grasslands where the Arabs roamed. I tried to lead them out.' My father sat down again and put his head in his hands, silenced for the moment overtaken by the memories.

At last he looked up with tears in his eyes and said sadly. 'It was terrible Edwin, I can still hear their screams, they were trapped against the valley cliffs there was no escape,' he groaned. 'I managed to rescue Sphere, she remembered me and trusted me to ride her out, and two fillies followed her. She may be their mother I don't know, the rest were too wild and too frightened to risk the fire. They ran back away from it, but the enemy threw more fire bolts down and it was all over for them.

That's why I sent for you instead of returning. We need Orion to repopulate the herd, give the people confidence to start again in the knowledge that the Arabs still remain for all time.'

'What about the farm, Dad?' I questioned, while walking over to the small paddock where Trian had released Orion. Leaning against the fence I watched him contentedly grazing.

'You're young and strong enough to manage that on your own Edwin,' he replied joining me. 'It's a good place to raise a family and I'd like to think I can return some time to see a grandson,' he jested thumping me hard on the back. 'Besides you need to buy another Arab now that Orion is staying here with me. Trian has explained the Quest family's responsibilities to the land I hope.'

'I might buy two,' I rejoined 'I've met Emily she's a wonderful girl Dad; we're getting married in October.'

'Well there you are then, no room for the old man I'd only be in the way.' He joked, 'No you go back Edwin,' he said more seriously. 'You know I'm alright, I will visit I promise. Now come and say hello to Sphere.'

He took me around to the other side of the cottage and in the rear paddock, Sphere trotted over looking for a titbit. The two fillies looked on curiously but didn't come near.

'They look healthy and contented enough,' I said

'We are waiting for the grass to recover and by autumn we should be able to release them back on to the plains. That's where they belong,' my father pronounced.

Returning to the table we sat drinking tankards of warm beer, not unlike my own home brew, reminiscing until the sun went down.

'It is time for you to return Edwin,' my father stated sadly. 'You must make it back during darkness. It is too dangerous to the land for anyone to see the gateway.'

I got up perplexed, trying not to get too emotional about leaving. Turning to the practical, I asked 'How am I to return without Orion?'

Trian will lend you Elsa; she knows the way and will return on her own. Ardenian ponies do not like to be away from the land.

115

And so I reluctantly retraced the way back through the kaleidoscopic tunnelled torrents of the falls and the ever thickening mists until I reached home. All the time remembering my father, leaving him waving stoically, myself saddened, that I had only found him again a few hours before. I will miss him dreadfully together with Orion, who helped me through my deepest depression. Now it is his fate to lead and increase the Ardenian herd. It is Dads and mine with Trian's help to keep the Quest responsibilities of guarding the gate and rearing Arabs on the lands behalf.

It is now two hours since I smacked Elsa fondly on the rump, watching her speed away disappearing into the mist.

I pour myself a whisky, turning the glass, the crystal reflecting the light of my sitting room fire, evoking the colours of the waterfall, the whisky glowing amber within. The clock chimes the half hour. It is now 11.30 pm and February 29th is almost over, I lift my glass and drink a toast to February 29th 2008.

The Joined-up Writers Group

After two years of tutor Ann Merrin's creative writing courses at Weston College in Nailsea, several members of the group were anxious not to lose all the stimulation and collaboration they had so enjoyed. So they began to meet regularly, over coffee at Waitrose in Portishead. Here they talked about writing and set each other more writing challenges, such as a poem on wind turbines and a 150 word story on the theme of vegetables! Watching manuscripts build up in desk drawers, they became even more determined not to see all this creativity going unnoticed.

Barbara, Pat, Naomi, and Patricia brought together fellow students from the course, and tutor, Ann, with the suggestion that they produce an anthology of their writing. And so the Joined-up Writers Group was formed.

'Acorns' is the group's first published collection. We hope that you enjoy reading the stories and poems as much as the group has enjoyed putting the collection together.

The Joined-up writers are:
Alan Becket; Barbara Calvert; Patricia Lloyd; Jane Mason; Ann Merrin; Maureen Nicholls; Naomi Stride; Pat Welford and Phil Whitehead.